Christmas
WITH ARTFUL OFFERINGS

**Delicious Cookie-Cutter Designs for
Quilting, Sewing, and Punchneedle**

Karina Hittle

Martingale®
& COMPANY

Christmas with Artful Offerings:
Delicious Cookie-Cutter Designs for Quilting,
Sewing, and Punchneedle
© 2007 by Karina Hittle

That Patchwork Place® is an imprint of Martingale & Company®.

Martingale & Company
20205 144th Ave. NE
Woodinville, WA 98072-8478 USA
www.martingale-pub.com

Printed in China
12 11 10 09 08 07   8 7 6 5 4 3 2 1

Library of Congress Cataloging-in-Publication Data
Library of Congress Control Number: 2007013332

ISBN: 978-1-56477-777-5

Credits

President & CEO: Tom Wierzbicki
Publisher: Jane Hamada
Editorial Director: Mary V. Green
Managing Editor: Tina Cook
Technical Editor: Dawn Anderson
Copy Editor: Melissa Bryan
Design Director: Stan Green
Assistant Design Director: Regina Girard
Illustrator: Laurel Strand
Cover & Text Designer: Shelly Garrison
Photographers: Bill Lindner & Brent Kane
Photo Assistant: Jason Lund
Photo Stylists: Dawn Anderson & Bridget Haugh

Dedication

To those who have inspired, taught, and assisted me in so many different ways over the years, but most especially to my dear husband, Audie, whose complete love and support, devotion, and encouragement is my most precious and cherished possession.
Thank you!

Mission Statement

Dedicated to providing quality products and service to inspire creativity.

CONTENTS

Introduction 4

Overview 4

Projects

Sugar Cookie Ornaments 7

Ginger Cookie Ornaments 11

Holly Button Plate Charger/Place Mat 15

Ginger Cookie Runner 17

Holly Button Tray/Place Mat 19

Sugar Cookie Runner 21

Ginger Cookie Mantel Village 23

Sugar Cookie Lined Apron 27

Peppermint Pinwheel Quilted Tablecloth 31

Peppermint Pinwheel Lined Dessert Napkins 35

Quilted Cookie Note Cards 37

Gingerbread Cookie Dough Tree 41

Sugar Cookie Christmas Tree 43

Cooling Cookies Wall Hanging 45

Cooling Cookies Pillow 47

Small Sugar Cookie Stocking 49

Gingerbread Stocking 51

Ginger Cookie Punchneedle Ornaments 55

Sugar Cookie Punchneedle Ornaments 59

Ginger Cookie Lined Apron 65

Sugar Cookie Vase 69

Patterns 71

Source Guide 94

About the Author 95

Acknowledgments 96

INTRODUCTION

OVERVIEW

Almost everyone has a favorite memory associated with Christmas and baking during the wonderful winter holiday season. Whether it's making sugar cookies and covering them with icing, or simply enjoying the sight and smell of gingerbread adorned with white piping and peppermints, something delicious happens when we experience these sensory delights.

This book introduces simple "recipes" for mixing up a batch of faux baked goods that look almost good enough to eat. Learning to bake hasn't been this much fun since you rolled out your very first cookie dough and used those well-worn cookie cutters to create your first culinary masterpiece.

With projects carefully selected to satisfy both the beginner and the experienced "baker," you'll easily move up the learning curve from simple sugar cookie ornaments to peppermint pinwheel napkins and a quilted cookie wall hanging.

For the more craft-minded bakers, a scrumptious selection of sugar cookie and gingerbread stockings, aprons, quilted note cards, and practical home-decorating items, such as table runners and even a vase, add a touch of "spice" to our baking menu.

Think of the materials list for each project as an ingredients list and the directions for each project as the recipe. For bakers who, like many of us, eventually want to experiment with slight variations from the original recipe, we offer a selection of punchneedle ornaments that are sure to hit the spot.

So pick a recipe or two, gather the proper ingredients, mix well, and . . . voilà! You've become a baking artist of the Artful Offerings kind!

For those inspired and delighted by a love of baking, one look at these scrumptious projects and you'll want to get started right away. Each project in *Christmas with Artful Offerings* was crafted with simplicity in mind. All you need are typical sewing notions, equipment, and techniques. For instance, while the "piped icing" on the cookies may look hand embroidered, it can easily be done with a tight zigzag or satin stitch on a traditional sewing machine. Or, if you do have an embroidery machine and software, simply scan the pattern into your computer and use it to create a machine-embroidery design that can be accommodated by typical hoop sizes on such machines.

In addition, the patterns are designed to help you gain experience and build toward subsequent projects. For example, the first few projects show you how to create delicious-looking faux sugar and ginger cookies. The next project provides instruction on how to create a plate charger or place mat, and then you learn how to combine all the previous elements to create a delightful table runner. The cookies are also incorporated into many other projects to make a mantelpiece decoration, tablecloth, wall hanging, aprons, decorative Christmas trees, holiday or greeting note cards, and a vase. Variations of these designs are also done as punchneedle patterns to further extend the theme and joy of faux baking.

With such a variety of designs and patterns, you'll be sure to "bake up" treats that all your friends and family will savor, year after year. Enjoy!

SPECIAL SUPPLIES

While there are many fine products you can use to complete the projects in this book, I have a few favorites. I like these quality items because they're easy to use, save time, and help me achieve professional results. For efficiency, the ingredients list with each project describes most materials in their generic form, but here I discuss some of my favorite products and the reasons I use them.

Hand overdyed wool: At our request, Miranda Weeks McGahey, president of Weeks Dye Works, created a new color for her hand overdyed wool collection specifically for this book. The new color is called Gingerbread #1234, and we think you're going to love it as much as we do. After listening carefully to what I was looking for, Miranda sent five scrumptious samples for my review, from which I ultimately selected the "gingerbread" for these projects. It was hard to choose, but I think you'll agree that the ginger cookies in this book look like they are freshly baked. Because Weeks Dye Works uses dye recipes, their rich, beautiful colors stay quite true from dye lot to dye lot. I love the thickness and feel of their wool and the tonal shade differences they achieve by overdyeing houndstooth, herringbone, and plain wools.

Wool felt: I discovered National Nonwovens WoolFelt about five years ago and have been using it ever since. I love its thickness, durability, and ease of use whether sewing by hand or machine. The palette of colors is also wonderful, ranging from soft to vibrant. This product can be used right off the bolt or easily felted to achieve a wide range of textures.

Spray adhesive and stabilizer: The Sulky KK 2000 product is a fantastic temporary spray adhesive. I can easily apply it in thin, even coats when I desire a pin-free solution, and the fabric will not shift during the sewing process. It's even safe to use with my sewing machines. Sulky Tear-Easy is a lightweight temporary tear-away stabilizer that I use to keep my stitches from distorting. I really like its versatility: depending on the project, I might use one or more layers of Tear-Easy and, when the stitching is completed, I can choose to remove all of the stabilizer or just the excess.

Interfacing: When I need a heavyweight stiff interfacing, I prefer using Timtex. It's easy to cut and provides firm support to any shape, yet I find that it remains soft and flexible enough to sew through by hand or machine.

Fusible webbing: Lite Steam-A-Seam and Lite Steam-A-Seam2 by the Warm Company are two fusible products I love using because they are lightweight and they don't become stiff, even after cooling. I also use the convenient tape, which comes in widths of ¼" and ½". This adhesive is pressure sensitive, giving me a temporary hold until I fuse it using a one-step ironing process that provides a permanent hold. Unfinished edges won't fray and it's so easy to use!

Batting: Warm & Natural 100%-cotton batting by the Warm Company is my favorite because the cotton is soft, flexible, and easy to quilt. I also like the fact that it's available in white and natural shades.

Buttons: I happened upon Just Another Button Company's unique and charming buttons in the Weeks Dye Works booth at my first quilt market. On display was a darling wool penny garland embellished with several handmade buttons. I fell in love with the popcorn buttons and made a mad dash to the Just Another Button Company booth to place my first order! I knew these little accents would be perfect for the projects in this book. I enjoy using these buttons because they come in an extensive variety of designs and sizes, they are handmade and durable, and the holes on even the tiniest buttons can easily accommodate the eye of a regular sewing needle. They are the perfect touch for embellishing and customizing your projects.

Ribbons and trimmings: I really like working with Bobbin Ribbon, Sweet Petites, and Pure Color ribbons by Morex Corporation. They are conveniently packaged on spools and come in a wide array of beautiful colors and eclectic styles.

Rickrack and pom-pom trimmings by Wrights add a sense of playful whimsy to my designs, and I use them often. The rickrack comes in several widths, from baby to jumbo. It's colorfast and has no-curl points. Both trimmings come in lots of fun colors ranging from traditional classics to vivid brights.

Cotton floss: DMC Corporation's six-strand cotton floss comes in hundreds of colorfast hues, so I can always find the perfect color. It's 100% cotton and the strands are easy to separate when preparing it for punching or stitching. The company's pearl cotton floss is also 100% colorfast cotton. A single strand of this floss makes buttonhole stitching quick and easy.

Sugar Cookie ORNAMENTS

Appearing to be fresh from the oven, these delicious-looking faux sugar cookies can adorn gifts, Christmas trees, and the Sugar Cookie Runner on page 21. One look and you're home for the holidays! This project provides the recipe for five different Sugar Cookie Ornaments: a Christmas Tree, Star, Bell, Swirl Ball, and Snowman. Enjoy!

FINISHED SIZE: APPROXIMATELY 5" X 5" (VARIES BY DESIGN)

INGREDIENTS

Yields 5 ornaments: Christmas Tree, Star, Bell, Swirl Ball, and Snowman.

½ yard of buttercream wool felt for cookie backgrounds

5" x 6" rectangle *each* of red, white, lemon, and light green wool felt for cookie icing

3½" x 3½" square *each* of baby blue and peacock wool felt for cookie icing

Scrap of orange wool felt for Snowman's nose

3½ yards of wired red-and-white gingham ribbon, ⅝" wide, for ornament hangers and bows

Embroidery thread to coordinate or contrast with each icing color and for piped icing

⅜ yard of tear-away stabilizer, 20" wide

Scrap of fusible web for Snowman's nose

1 skein of chocolate brown cotton floss (DMC #898) for Snowman's eyes

Seam sealant

Fine-tipped permanent marker

Removable fabric marker

Freezer paper

Temporary spray adhesive

CUTTING

From the red-and-white gingham ribbon, cut:

5 pieces, 22½" long; cut each end into a dovetail (V shape) and apply seam sealant to the cut edges

PATTERN PREPARATION

Follow these steps for each ornament, using the patterns on pages 71–73. The Swirl Ball ornament is illustrated here as an example.

1. Using the marker, trace the outer line of each sugar cookie pattern, the reverse image, and the icing pattern onto the *uncoated* side of the freezer paper. Cut on the marked lines.

7

2. Using a *dry* iron, press the freezer-paper patterns, *shiny* side down, onto the right side of the wool felt. Cut out the sugar cookie, the reverse sugar cookie, and the icing shapes. Set aside.

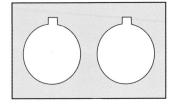

PIPED ICING

1. For each ornament, cut a piece of tear-away stabilizer larger than the icing cutout. Trace the piped icing design and dashed placement line onto the stabilizer, using the piped icing guide provided with the ornament pattern. *Note that the piped icing patterns are reversed.*

2. Lightly apply spray adhesive to the back of the stabilizer pattern. Adhere the stabilizer to the back of the icing cutout, aligning the dashed line with the outer edges of the cutout. Straight stitch along all piped icing design lines.

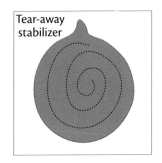

Tear-away stabilizer

3. Flip the icing over so that the front side faces up. Satin stitch directly on top of the straight-stitched lines. Pull the thread tails to the back side. Knot and trim the excess thread. Remove the excess stabilizer.

4. For the Snowman, cut one carrot nose from fusible-web-backed orange felt, using the pattern on page 73. Fuse the carrot nose to the snowman's face, following the manufacturer's directions. Stitch close to the edges of the nose.

ASSEMBLY

1. Center the icing, right side up, on the corresponding cookie shape. Using a straight stitch, sew close to the edge of the icing.

2. For the Snowman, refer to the pattern as a guide and use a fabric marker to make dots for eye placement on the face. Using six strands of floss, make a French knot for each eye.

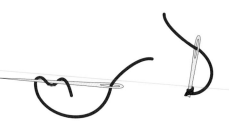

French knot

3. Fold the wired ribbon in half. Lightly apply spray adhesive to the back of the ornament front. Sandwich the ornament front and back pieces, wrong sides together, inserting the center fold of the ribbon ½" inside the cutouts at the top center.

4. Straight stitch around the ornament pieces close to the cut edges.

5. Tie the ribbon into a bow, leaving a small loop near the top edge of the ornament for hanging.

Ginger Cookie ORNAMENTS

Looking taste-temptingly good, these faux gingerbread cookies are sure to delight in a wide variety of roles, from ornaments to package tags to framed fabric art for display. You can create a cookie community complete with Church, Row House, Bungalow, and Pine Tree, or mix up a flurry of ginger cookie Snowflakes for family and friends. They also make wonderful adornments for the Ginger Cookie Runner on page 17, the Peppermint Pinwheel Quilted Tablecloth on page 31, and the Ginger Cookie Lined Apron on page 65, bringing a festive holiday feeling to brighten any day. Enjoy them hot off the sewing machine with your favorite beverage for a gratifying treat!

FINISHED SIZE: APPROXIMATELY 4" X 4" TO 5" X 8" (VARIES BY DESIGN)

INGREDIENTS

Yields either 4 Village ornaments or 10 Snowflake ornaments. Depending on the actual size of your wool fat quarter and the placement of your patterns, you might be able to cut more ornaments or different combinations from a single fat quarter.

1 fat quarter of gingerbread-colored hand-dyed wool

⅝ yard of fusible web, 18" wide

½ yard of tear-away stabilizer, 20" wide

Red-and-white striped ribbon, ⅜" wide (2 yards are needed for 4 Village ornaments and 5 yards are needed for 10 Snowflake ornaments)

White embroidery thread for piped icing

Seam sealant

Fine-tipped permanent marker

Freezer paper

Temporary spray adhesive

Teflon pressing sheet

CUTTING

From the red-and-white striped ribbon, cut:

1 piece, 18" long, for each ornament (4 for Village ornaments or 10 for Snowflake ornaments); cut each end at an angle and apply seam sealant to the cut edges

PATTERN PREPARATION

The following instructions are for four Village ornaments. The Pine Tree is illustrated here as an example. Make the Snowflake ornaments in the same manner, using these directions as a guide. Patterns are on pages 74–78.

1. Apply fusible web to the back of the wool, following the manufacturer's directions. *Do not* remove the paper backing at this time.

2. Using the marker, trace the outline of each cookie pattern once onto the *uncoated* side of the freezer paper. Cut on the marked lines.

3. Using a *dry* iron, press the freezer-paper patterns, *shiny* side down, onto the right side of the wool. Cut out the ginger cookie shapes. Set aside.

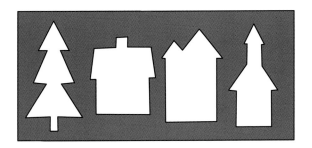

PIPED ICING

1. For each ornament, cut a piece of tear-away stabilizer larger than the cookie cutout. Trace the piped icing design and dashed placement line onto the stabilizer, using the piped icing guide provided with the ornament pattern. *Note that the icing patterns are reversed.*

2. Remove the paper backing from the cookie cutout. Place the tear-away stabilizer on the back side of the cutout, aligning the dashed line with the outer edges of the cutout. *Do not* iron the tear-away stabilizer to the cutout. Straight stitch along all icing design lines.

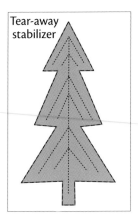

Tear-away stabilizer

3. Flip the cookie over so that the front side faces up. Satin stitch directly on top of the straight-stitched lines. Pull the thread tails to the back side.

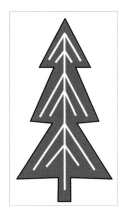

4. Remove the excess stabilizer. Place the cookie cutout face up on a pressing sheet and press to fuse the thread tails to the back of the cutout. Let cool completely and lift the cutout off the pressing sheet. This process fuses the thread tails to prevent raveling.

Pressing sheet

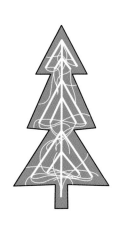

5. Cut away the excess thread tails.

ASSEMBLY

1. Place the remaining wool, paper side up, on a flat work surface. Remove the paper backing.

2. Put the ornament fronts, sticky side down, on the wool. Cut the backing piece even with the edges of the front piece. Cutting the backing to match the front, rather than using the template, will accommodate any shrinkage of the front that occurred during the satin-stitching process.

3. Fold each length of ribbon in half. Sandwich the ornament front and back pieces together, inserting the center fold of the ribbon ½" inside the cutouts at the top center.

4. Straight stitch around the ornament pieces close to the cut edges.

5. Tie the ribbon into a decorative knot, approximately 2" above the ornament top, letting the ends hang loosely. These ornaments are ready to hang!

Holly Button
PLATE CHARGER/PLACE MAT

The term "plate charger" evolved from an early English use of the word "charge" as in to "charge" or fill up one's plate. Eventually the term came to mean a decorative plate placed under a salad or dinner plate. These ornate plate chargers created from layers of wool, wool felt, and fabric can function as traditional chargers in a formal setting when used in combination with a tablecloth, or as place mats in a more casual environment.

FINISHED SIZE: 13" X 13"

INGREDIENTS

Yields 2 plate chargers or place mats.

½ yard of bright red wool felt for bottom layer

½ yard of white wool felt for middle layer

⅜ yard of cream cotton fabric for top layer

⅜ yard of fusible web, 18" wide

½ yard of tear-away stabilizer, 20" wide

Red embroidery thread for satin stitching

White thread for construction

4 large holly buttons (Just Another Button Company)

Fine-tipped permanent marker

Freezer paper

Temporary spray adhesive

PATTERN PREPARATION

1. Apply fusible web to the back of the cream cotton. Set aside.

2. Follow the directions on page 81 to make the Plate Charger/Place Mat pattern. Using the marker, trace one pattern each for the bottom, middle, and top layers of the Plate Charger/ Place Mat onto the *uncoated* side of the freezer paper. Cut along the marked cutting lines to make the three patterns.

3. Using a *dry* iron, press the freezer-paper patterns, *shiny* side down, onto the right side of the corresponding fabrics. Cut out the shapes carefully. Do not discard the center cutout from the cream top layer; it will be used in a later step as a liner to prevent the red wool from showing through the white wool.

4. Using the patterns created in step 2, repeat step 3 to cut out a second plate charger/place mat.

ASSEMBLY

1. For each charger, center and fuse the cream cotton top layer to the white felt middle layer.

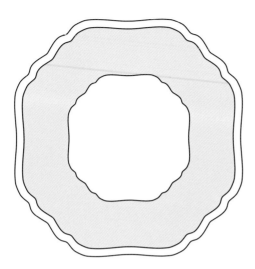

2. Place the fused top and middle layers, right side down, on a flat work surface. Carefully center and fuse the reserved center cutout from the top layer onto the back of the middle layer.

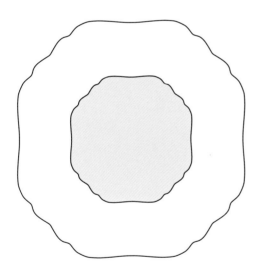

3. Turn the partial charger right side up. Place a piece of tear-away stabilizer, cut slightly larger than the middle layer, under the unit. Use red thread to satin stitch around the raw edges of the cotton fabric, and then remove the excess stabilizer.

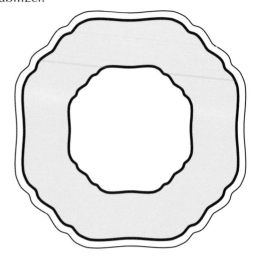

Note: If desired, and depending on your machine, sew another layer of satin stitching over the original layer so the fabric edge does not show through.

4. Apply spray adhesive to the back of the middle layer and center it, sticky side down, over the red felt bottom layer.

5. Use white thread to straight stitch close to the cut edge of the middle layer. Sew two large holly buttons to the upper-left corner of the charger.

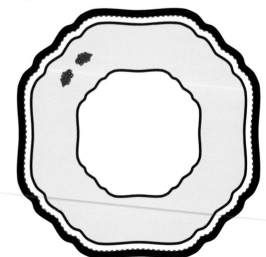

Ginger Cookie Runner

Modify the Holly Button Plate Charger/ Place Mat to create a darling runner for a kitchen island or dining table. Stitch tempting ginger cookies in place to create a permanent decoration, or simply place loose cookie ornaments on top of the three chargers to provide removable treats for a post-dinner tree-trimming party.

To make the runner shown here, refer to the instructions for the Ginger Cookie Ornaments (page 11) and create only the cookie fronts for two Pine Trees, two Bungalows, and five Snowflakes. Assemble the top and middle layers of three plate chargers/place mats (pages 15–16). Arrange and fuse the cookie fronts over the three partially assembled chargers and stitch in place with narrow zigzag stitches. Lay the three bottom charger pieces in a row, spacing them 6" apart. Center a 2-yard length of 4⅜"-wide holly print ribbon over the top, and then center the embellished charger tops over the bottom layers, sandwiching the ribbon in between. Pin and then stitch close to the edge of the middle charger layer to secure. Trim the ends of the ribbon into a dovetail (V shape) and apply seam sealant to the cut edges.

Holly Button TRAY/PLACE MAT

Optional display ideas for this cookie tray are limited only by your creativity. Try hanging a tray or two from wide ribbon tails topped with one large festive bow to make a unique wall hanging. These trays can also be used as penniless penny rugs or combined as a table runner (see page 21).

FINISHED SIZE: APPROXIMATELY 10" X 16⅞"

INGREDIENTS

Yields 2 trays/place mats.

⅜ yard of white wool felt for bottom layer

⅜ yard of bright red wool felt for middle layer

1 fat quarter of houndstooth hand-dyed wool for top layer

⅝ yard of fusible web, 18" wide

½ yard of tear-away stabilizer, 20" wide

White embroidery thread for satin stitching

Red thread for construction

4 large holly buttons (Just Another Button Company)

Fine-tipped permanent marker

Freezer paper

Temporary spray adhesive

PATTERN PREPARATION

1. Apply fusible web to the back side of the houndstooth wool. Set aside.

2. Follow the directions on page 82 to make the Tray/Place Mat pattern. Using the marker, trace one pattern each for the bottom, middle, and top layers of the tray/place mat onto the uncoated side of the freezer paper. Cut along the marked cutting lines to make the three patterns.

3. Iron the freezer paper patterns *shiny* side down onto the right side of the corresponding fabrics using a *dry* iron, and then cut out the shapes. Keep the center cutout from the houndstooth check in your wool stash for a future use.

4. Using the patterns created in step 2, repeat step 3 to cut out a second tray/place mat.

ASSEMBLY

1. For each tray, center and fuse the houndstooth top layer to the red felt middle layer.

2. Place a piece of tear-away stabilizer, cut slightly larger than the middle layer, under the partial tray. Use white thread to satin stitch around the raw edges of the houndstooth wool, and then remove the excess stabilizer.

Note: If desired, and depending on your machine, sew another layer of satin stitching over the original layer so the wool edge does not show through.

4. Sew two large holly buttons to the upper-right corner of the tray.

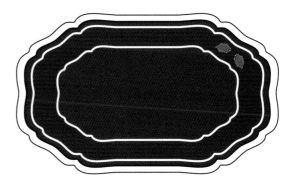

3. Apply spray adhesive to the back of the middle layer and center it, sticky side down, over the white felt bottom layer. Use red thread to straight stitch close to the cut edge of the middle layer.

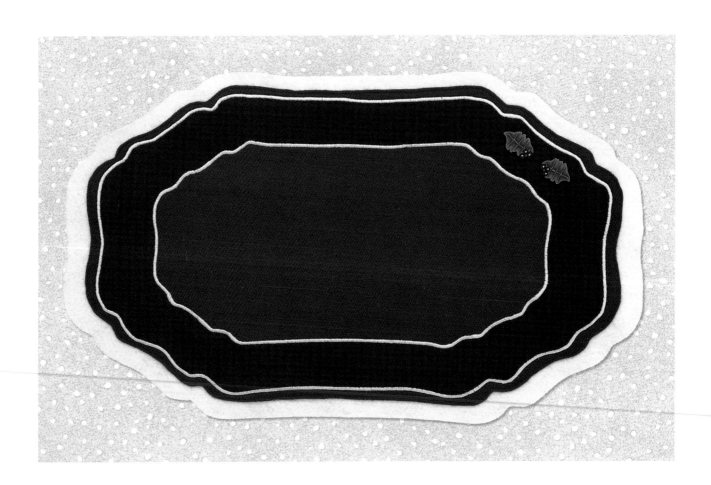

Sugar Cookie Runner

The Holly Button Tray/Place Mat project can easily be transformed into a unique table runner that can decorate your dining table or adorn a console. The Sugar Cookie Ornaments (page 7) are substituted for the holly buttons as embellishments. For a permanent decoration, make the cookie fronts only and stitch them in place on the runner. Or for a temporary embellishment, simply lay completed ornaments over the surface of the runner during the dinner celebration, then give them as party favors to departing dinner guests.

To make the charming table runner shown here, assemble the top and middle layers of two trays/place mats (pages 19–20), but don't attach them to the bottom layer. For permanent sugar cookie embellishments, refer to Sugar Cookie Ornaments (page 7) and make the fronts only for one Swirl Ball, one Snowman, one Christmas Tree, one Bell, and one Star. Then arrange and fuse the cookie fronts to the partially assembled place mats and stitch in place close to the outer edges of the cookies. Lay the two bottom layers of the mats on a flat surface 6" apart and center a 60" length of 4³⁄₈"-wide holly print ribbon over the top. Then center the cookie-embellished pieces over the bottom layers, sandwiching the ribbon in between. Pin and then stitch close to the edge of the middle place mat layer to secure. Trim the ends of the ribbon into a dovetail (V shape) and apply seam sealant to the cut edges.

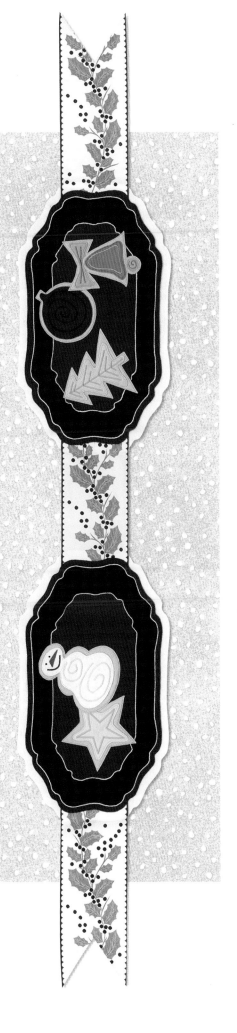

Ginger Cookie MANTEL VILLAGE

For instant holiday decorating, simply unfold this peaceful
holiday village and place it on a mantel or table. Add some pinecones
and greens and your decorating is complete. When the holidays have
come to an end, fold and store your village flat until next year!

FINISHED SIZE: APPROXIMATELY 12½" X 42"

INGREDIENTS

Yields 1 village.

- 1⅓ yards of blue snowy-sky-motif fabric for sky
  (or ¾ yard if the usable width of the fabric is at
  least 42½" wide)

- 1⅓ yards of ivory tonal-swirl-motif fabric for snow-
  covered ground (or ⅛ yard if the usable width of
  the fabric is at least 42½" wide)

- 1 fat quarter of gingerbread-colored hand-dyed
  wool for village

- ⅝ yard of fusible web, 18" wide

- 1⅜ yards of tear-away stabilizer, 20" wide

- Embroidery thread for satin stitching

- Thread for construction

- Fine-tipped permanent marker

- Freezer paper

- Temporary spray adhesive

- 1¼ yards of heavyweight stiff interfacing, 13" wide

CUTTING

From the blue fabric, cut:
1 strip, 23½" x 42½"

From the ivory fabric, cut:
1 strip, 3" x 42½"

From the heavyweight stiff interfacing, cut:
7 rectangles, 5½" x 12⅛"

GINGER COOKIE RECIPE

Cut a 13" x 43" strip from the stabilizer. Set aside
until step 5 on page 24. Prepare the Ginger Cookie
Ornaments (fronts only), using the instructions for
"Pattern Preparation" and "Piped Icing" on pages
11–12 as a guide. Make one Church, one Row
House and one reverse Row House, one Bungalow
and one reverse Bungalow, one Pine Tree and one
reverse Pine Tree. Set aside.

ASSEMBLY

1. Pin the snow fabric to the sky fabric along a
   42½" edge, with right sides together and edges
   aligned. Using a ¼" seam allowance, stitch the
   pieces together and press the seam toward the
   sky fabric.

2. Center and fuse the Church 1¼" from the
   bottom edge of the background rectangle.

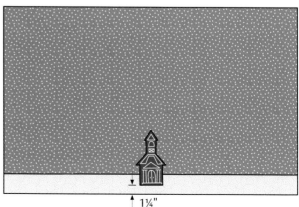

1¼"

3. Measuring from the center of the Church, pin-mark the fabric on each side of the center every 6". Center the remaining cookies at the pin marks so that the two sides are mirror images.

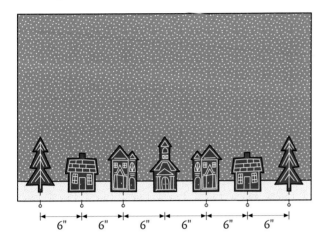

4. Fuse the remaining cookie fronts in place. Remove the pins. Lay the piece facedown on a flat work surface.

5. Lightly spray one side of the 13" x 43" strip of stabilizer with spray adhesive. Adhere the stabilizer, sticky side down, to the back of the background rectangle, covering the lower half of the fabric.

6. Flip the background rectangle right side up. Zigzag stitch around all cut edges of the ginger cookie cutouts using a narrow stitch width. Turn the piece over and carefully remove the stabilizer.

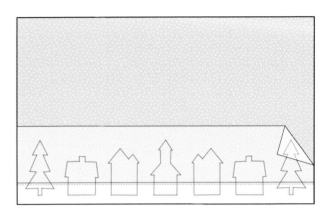

7. Fold ½" of the top and bottom edges to the wrong side and press. Fold the background rectangle in half lengthwise, right sides together, and pin the side seams. Sew a ¼" seam along the side edges.

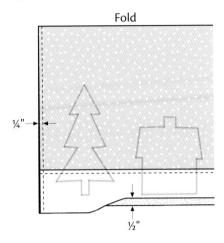

Fold

¼"

½"

8. Turn the rectangle right side out and press.

9. Begin measuring from the left edge and draw six vertical lines, 6" apart, across the village panel. Extend the lines from the top of the panel to the bottom, between the ginger cookie cutouts. Stitch on the drawn lines with coordinating thread.

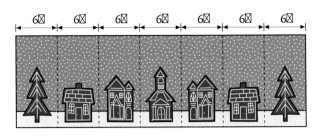

6" 6" 6" 6" 6" 6" 6"

10. Insert the rectangles of heavyweight stiff interfacing into the bottom opening of each ginger cookie section, carefully aligning them with the bottom edges of the panel.

11. Pin the bottom openings closed through all layers. Stitch across the bottom of the panel, close to the edge.

Sugar Cookie LINED APRON

Add style and fun to your baking day by wearing
this "sweet" waist apron. Keep your recipe cards close at hand
in the pocket, which is decorated with a sugar cookie motif.

FINISHED SIZE: GATHERS TO 18½" AT THE WAIST WITH A 20" LENGTH

INGREDIENTS

Yields 1 apron.

2¼ yards of red-and-ivory striped cotton fabric

1½ yards (1 package) of red jumbo (¾"-wide) rick-rack

5" x 5" square of buttercream wool felt for sugar cookie background

4" x 5" rectangle of red wool felt for sugar cookie icing

¼ yard of tear-away stabilizer, 20" wide

Embroidery thread for piped icing

Thread for construction

½ yard of green grosgrain ribbon, ⅝" wide (if making the apron with the Swirl Ball ornament on the pocket)

1½ yards of fusible-web tape, ¼" wide

Fine-tipped permanent marker

Seam sealant

Freezer paper

Temporary spray adhesive

Teflon pressing sheet

Safety pin

CUTTING

Pay attention to the direction of the stripes on each fabric piece when cutting.

From the red-and-ivory striped fabric, cut:
One rectangle, 35" x 40"

One strip, 5" x 72"

One rectangle, 8" x 18"

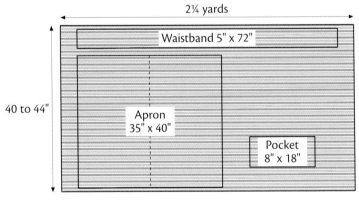

Cutting guide

SUGAR COOKIE RECIPE

Prepare the Swirl Ball or other cookie ornament of your choice (front only) using the instructions on pages 7–8 as a guide. Set aside.

Pocket Cookie and Rickrack Options

If you plan to feature a different sugar cookie on the apron pocket, be sure to select a coordinating color of rickrack.

 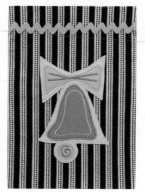 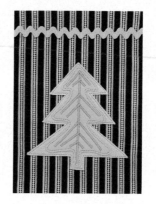 

POCKET

1. Fold the 8" x 18" pocket piece in half and press along the fold line. Unfold the piece and set aside. Cut one 9" length of rickrack. Iron a strip of fusible-web tape to the back of the rick-rack. *Tip: To avoid scorching the rickrack, use a pressing sheet.* Remove the paper backing and fuse the rickrack to the pocket piece 1½" from the fold line. Straight stitch the rickrack in place.

2. Spray the back of the completed sugar cookie front with spray adhesive. Center the cookie on the pocket between the rickrack and the bottom of the pocket. Straight stitch the cookie in place, stitching close to the cut edge of the shape.

3. Fold the pocket in half, right sides together. You now have an 8" x 9" rectangle. Sew ¼" from the raw edges, leaving a 2" opening on the bottom. Trim the excess rickrack.

4. Turn the pocket right side out. Press the pocket, making sure to turn under the raw edges of the 2" opening when pressing.

5. If using the Swirl Ball ornament design on the pocket, make a bow using the ½-yard piece of ribbon. Cut dovetails at the ends, apply seam sealant to the cut edges, and use a safety pin to attach the bow just above the sugar cookie ornament.

   Note: Remove the bow when washing the apron.

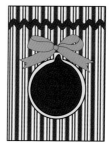

APRON AND LINING

1. Fold the apron rectangle in half, wrong sides together, to make a 20" x 35" rectangle with the stripes running vertically. Press along the fold line. Unfold and set aside. Cut one 35" length of rickrack. Iron a strip of fusible-web tape to the back of the rickrack. Remove the paper backing and fuse the rickrack to the apron piece, 2" from the fold line. Straight stitch the rickrack in place.

2. Fold the rectangle in half, right sides together, along the fold line. Sew a ¼" seam on both 20" edges. Trim the excess rickrack.

3. Turn the apron right side out and press flat. Pin the pocket to the apron approximately 6" from the left side and 6" from the folded bottom edge. If desired, align the stripes on the pocket with the stripes on the apron.

4. Leaving the top edge of the pocket open, topstitch the pocket in place ⅛" from the remaining three edges.

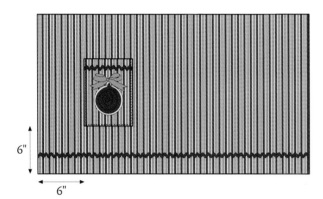

6"

6"

5. Stitch a basting stitch through all layers, ¼" and ½" from the top raw edges of the lined apron piece. Pull the threads to gather the top edge of the apron to a width of 18½". Set aside.

WAISTBAND

1. Fold the ends of the 5" x 72" waistband strip in ½" and press.

2. Fold the strip in half lengthwise, wrong sides together. Press.

3. Open the pressed waistband. Fold the raw edges to the center, and re-press with the iron.

4. With a pin, mark the center of the waistband. With two more pins, mark 9¼" to the left and right of the center pin. Remove the center pin. You now have an 18½" opening between the two pins.

5. Sandwich and pin the gathered edge of the lined apron piece between the pins on the waistband. Starting at one end of the waistband, topstitch ¼" from the folded edges of the strip, making sure each side of the waistband strip is caught when stitched together.

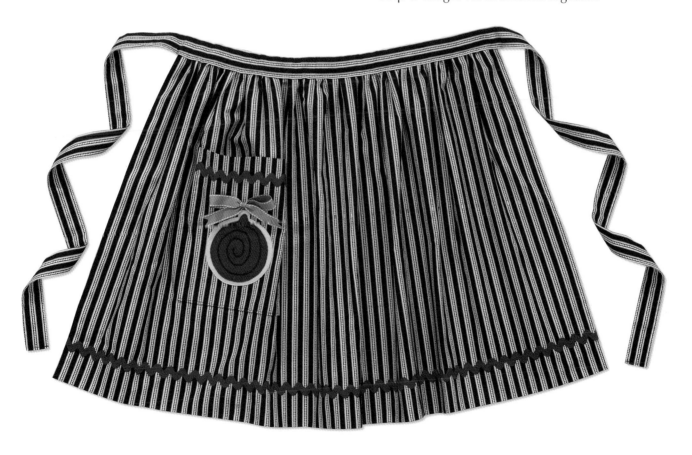

Peppermint Pinwheel
QUILTED TABLECLOTH

Peppermint candy is said to have been invented in Austria in 1927 when a gentleman named Eduard Haas III combined pressed sugar with peppermint oil to create a tasty treat. Today peppermint, frequently shown as a bright red-and-white swirl or stripe, is used to adorn a wide variety of edible and decorative goods. Start a new tradition this year by displaying your holiday baked goods on this small peppermint-inspired quilted tablecloth featuring removable ginger cookie ornaments. After enjoying your culinary endeavors, relax and enjoy decorating a Christmas tree with the ginger cookie snowflake ornaments.

FINISHED SIZE: APPROXIMATELY 37" X 37"

INGREDIENTS

Yields 1 tablecloth. Use prewashed fabric.

1⅝ yards of red cotton fabric for blocks and backing

⅞ yard of ivory cotton fabric for blocks and borders

⅞ yard of brown cotton fabric for sashing and binding

2 fat quarters of gingerbread-colored wool for ginger cookies

42" x 42" piece of cotton batting

⅝ yard of fusible web, 18" wide

⅝ yard of tear-away stabilizer, 20" wide

2¼ yards of hunter green ribbon, ⅛" wide

White embroidery thread for piped icing

Thread for construction

12 large holly sprig buttons (Just Another Button Company)

Fine-tipped permanent marker

Freezer paper

Temporary spray adhesive

Fabric marker

See-through ruler

Marking pencil

CUTTING

From the ivory cotton, cut:

2 strips, 5" x width of fabric; crosscut into 16 squares, 5" x 5"

2 strips, 8½" x width of fabric; crosscut into 4 strips, 8½" x 17½"

From the red cotton, cut:

2 strips, 5" x width of fabric; crosscut into 16 squares, 5" x 5"

1 square, 42" x 42"

From the cotton batting, cut:

1 square, 42" x 42"

From the brown cotton, cut:

5 strips, 1½" x width of fabric. Crosscut into 6 strips, 1½" x 8½"; 3 strips, 1½" x 17½"; and 2 strips 1½" x 35½".

4 strips, 4½" x width of fabric

From the green ribbon, cut:

12 pieces, 6" long

GINGER COOKIE RECIPE

Following the project instructions on pages 11–13, prepare 12 Ginger Cookie Snowflake Ornaments (4 of each design). For the ornament hangers, fold the 6" lengths of green ribbon in half, inserting the cut ends between the cookie fronts and backs before final assembly. Set aside.

PEPPERMINT PINWHEEL BLOCK

All seam allowances are ¼" unless otherwise stated.

1. Layer the ivory squares over the red squares, right sides together and edges even. Using a fabric marker, draw a diagonal line across all ivory squares. Straight stitch ¼" to the left and right

sides of the marked line. Cut on the marked line. Press the seam allowances toward the red fabric.

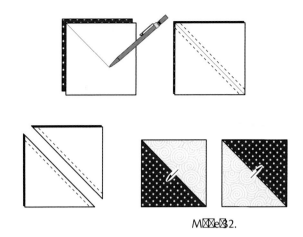

Make 32.

2. Using a Bias Square® ruler, trim each half-square-triangle unit to 4½" x 4½". Place the diagonal line of the ruler along the seam line of the unit and trim the two sides. Rotate the unit and trim the remaining two sides. Make 32.

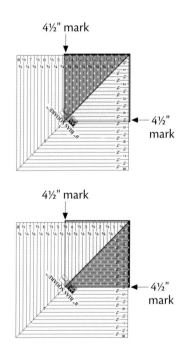

3. With right sides together, sew half-square-triangle units into pairs as shown.

Make 16.

4. Sew two pairs of half-square-triangle units together as shown to make an 8½" Pinwheel block.

Make 8.

QUILT-TOP ASSEMBLY

1. Sew two Pinwheel blocks to a 1½" x 8½" sashing strip as shown. Press toward the sashing strip. Make two.

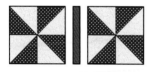

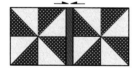

Make 2.

2. Join the two units from step 1 with a 1½" x 17½" sashing strip as shown to make the center unit for the tablecloth. Press toward the sashing.

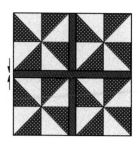

Make 1.

3. Sew a 1½" x 17½" sashing strip to opposite sides of the center unit. Sew an 8½" x 17½" border strip to each side sashing strip. Press toward the sashing. Set aside.

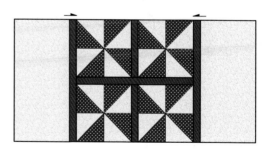

4. Sew a 1½" x 8½" sashing strip to one side of a Pinwheel block. Repeat for a second Pinwheel block. Sew the sashed blocks to the ends of an 8½" x 17½" border strip as shown to make the top border strip. Repeat for the bottom border strip. Press toward the sashing.

Make 2.

5. Sew a 1½" x 35½" sashing strip to each of the border strips from step 4.

Make 2.

6. With right sides together, pin the sashing side of the top and bottom border strips to the pinwheel center unit with side borders. Stitch and then press seam allowances toward the borders.

QUILT ASSEMBLY

1. Lay the quilt backing wrong side up on a flat work surface and apply a coat of spray adhesive. Layer the cotton batting on top of the backing, matching all edges, and smooth out any wrinkles.

2. Spray the back of the quilt top with spray adhesive and center over the batting and backing layers. The batting and backing will be about 3" larger on all sides than the quilt top.

3. Quilt using your favorite technique.

4. Use a fabric marker and see-through ruler to square up the corners and sides by marking, not cutting, a line around the entire quilt top.

5. Draw a line ½" in from the line marked in step 4, using the see-through ruler as a guide. Trim the excess batting and backing by cutting on the outer marked line. This is done so that the binding width will match the sashing width.

6. Fold the 4½"-wide brown binding strips in half lengthwise. Press.

7. Align the raw edges of a binding strip with the marked edge on one side of the quilt top and pin.

8. Sew the binding strip in place. Press the binding strip away from the quilt top and trim any excess. Stitch a binding strip to the opposite side of the quilt top in the same manner.

9. Stitch binding strips to the top and bottom edges of the quilt in the same manner as for the sides.

10. Fold the side binding strips to the back of the quilt so that the edge of the binding meets the stitching line, and pin in place. Repeat for the top and bottom binding strips. Whipstitch the binding to the quilt back.

FINISHING TOUCHES

1. Center and sew three holly sprig buttons ¾" from the sashing along the center section of each border.

2. Using the green ribbon, hang a completed ornament from each button.

Peppermint Pinwheel Lined Dessert Napkins

Border a single Peppermint Pinwheel block with 1½"-wide brown strips to make a napkin that matches the tablecloth. To finish, cut a 10½" square of matching brown fabric. Stitch it right sides together to the bordered Pinwheel block, leaving an opening for turning. Turn right side out and slipstitch the opening closed. Sew a large holly sprig button to one corner and presto . . . matching napkins!

Quilted Cookie NOTE CARDS

Note cards are a great way to stay in touch. Use these delightful quilted cards for favorite recipes, holiday notes and poems, or gift cards. Display them on small easels to add holiday cheer to any nook or cranny. Add an optional grommet to a top corner, run a pretty ribbon through the hole, and it's ready to hang on any tree or decorate a wrapped gift. Quilted note cards are perfect for using up any scraps of fabric, wool, and wool felt you may have left over from other projects.

FINISHED SIZE: 6" X 8¾"

Note card front and back

INGREDIENTS

Yields 1 quilted note card.

6" x 15" piece of print fabric for card front and back pocket

6" x 9" piece of contrasting print for card back

6" x 9" piece of heavyweight stiff interfacing

2¼" x 36" strip of contrasting print for binding

¼ yard of fusible web, 18" wide

¼ yard of tear-away stabilizer, 20" wide

Embroidery thread

Fine-tipped permanent marker

Freezer paper

Temporary spray adhesive

Walking foot (optional)

Christmas Star

6" x 6" square of buttercream wool felt

5" x 5" square of lemon wool felt

5 popcorn buttons (Just Another Button Company): 1 large, 2 medium, and 2 small

9" length of pine garland

Holiday Bell

5" x 6" rectangle of buttercream wool felt

3½" x 3½" square *each* of baby blue and peacock wool felt

5 sleigh bell buttons (Just Another Button Company): 1 large, 2 medium, and 2 small

9" length of pine garland

Ginger Cookie Snowflake

5" x 5" square of gingerbread-colored hand-dyed wool

2 small red-and-white swirl buttons and 3 large peppermint buttons (Just Another Button Company)

12" length of pine garland

Ginger Cookie Bungalow

6" x 7" rectangle of gingerbread-colored wool

5 golden star buttons (Just Another Button Company): 3 extra-large and 2 large

9" length of pine garland

COOKIE RECIPES

Prepare the desired Sugar Cookie or Ginger Cookie Ornament (front only). For the Star or Bell, follow the sugar cookie instructions on pages 7–8 as a guide. For the Bungalow or Snowflake, follow the ginger cookie instructions for "Pattern Preparation" and "Piped Icing" on pages 11–12 as a guide. Set the prepared cookie front aside.

FRONT CONSTRUCTION

1. Cut the 6" x 15" rectangle for the card front and back pocket into a 6" x 9" rectangle for the front and a 6" square for the pocket. Apply spray adhesive to the back of the card front. Place the piece, sticky side down, on the rectangle of heavyweight stiff interfacing, matching the edges and smoothing out any wrinkles.

2. Beginning on an outside edge, echo quilt the rectangle shape, spacing the lines 1" apart until you come to the center of the rectangle. Pull the thread tails to the back and tie off.

3. If using a Sugar Cookie Ornament, apply spray adhesive to the back of the ornament and center the cookie on the front of the quilted note card, approximately 1½" from the bottom of the card. If using a Ginger Cookie Ornament, fuse the ornament in place.

4. Stitch the cookie cutout onto the quilted note card close to the cut edge. *Tip: I used a straight stitch on the wool felt sugar cookies and a small zigzag stitch on the wool ginger cookies.*

5. Shape a piece of the pine rope garland. Whipstitch the garland to the note card, centering it approximately ¾" from the top of the card.

6. Sew the five decorative buttons to the lower edge of the garland, starting with the center button and then evenly spacing the remaining four buttons as shown in the project photo.

BACK CONSTRUCTION

1. Apply fusible web to the back of the fabric for the note card back. Carefully fuse the back piece to the back of the note card front. To avoid melting the garland and buttons, be careful not to use excessive heat.

2. Fold the 6" pocket square in half, wrong sides together. Pin the pocket to the back of the note card, aligning the raw edges at the sides and bottom. Baste the pocket to the back of the note card, ⅛" from the raw edges.

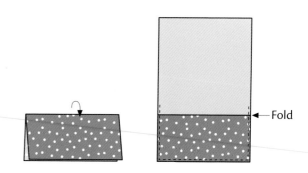

Fold

BINDING THE CARD

1. Cut the binding strip in half to make two 2¼" x 18" strips. Fold the strips in half lengthwise, wrong sides together, and press.

2. Align the raw edges of one binding strip with one long edge of the quilted note card front. Pin. Repeat on the opposite side.

3. Sew the binding strips to the note card, making sure to catch the pocket edges. Press the binding away from the card. Trim excess.

4. Repeat steps 2 and 3 for the top and bottom edges of the note card. Fold the side binding to the back of the note card so that the edge of the binding meets the stitching line, and pin in place. Repeat for the top and bottom bindings. Whipstitch the binding to the back of the note card.

Gingerbread COOKIE DOUGH TREE

Decorating for the holidays sweetens every room in the house, especially the kitchen! This simple tree leaves plenty of room for decorating with lots of candylike buttons, rickrack, and decorative stitching. By adding a cinnamon stick trunk, you can "plant" this deliciously distinctive-looking tree in an earthenware mixing bowl to make a sweet, showstopping table centerpiece with height. Fill the bowl with red berries and greenery for a spectacular finishing touch.

FINISHED SIZE: APPROXIMATELY 16" X 9½" DIAMETER AT FULLEST PART

INGREDIENTS

Yields 1 tree.

⅝ yard of hazelnut-colored wool felt for tree lining

1 fat quarter of gingerbread-colored hand-dyed wool for tree slipcover

2¼ yards (1 package) of white medium (½"-wide) rickrack

⅞ yard of white pom-pom fringe

2 yards of fusible-web tape, ¼" wide

1 yard of fusible web, 18" wide

Buttons (Just Another Button Company)
- 12 extra-large tea-stained stars
- 12 medium heart cookies
- 12 medium lime-and-white swirls

Embroidery thread for decorative stitching and attaching rickrack

Freezer paper

Teflon pressing sheet

9" x 4" craft cone

½" wooden dowel, 21" long

Brown craft paint

6 or 7 cinnamon sticks, 12" long

Mixing bowl

Red berries and evergreen sprigs

Dry floral foam

Hot-glue gun and glue sticks

PATTERN PREPARATION

1. Apply fusible web to the back of both the wool felt and hand-dyed wool. *Do not* remove the paper backing at this time.

2. Make the pattern as indicated on page 83. Trace the full-size assembled pattern, including dotted garland placement lines, onto the *uncoated* side of freezer paper. Then, using the freezer-paper pattern, trace all lines onto a piece of tear-away stabilizer cut larger than the pattern. Set the stabilizer aside.

3. Using a *dry* iron, press the freezer-paper pattern, *shiny* side down, to the right side of the wool. Cut along the outside lines. Remove the pattern and iron it *shiny* side down to the felt, using a dry iron. Cut along the outside lines.

SLIPCOVER ASSEMBLY

1. Remove the paper backing from the back of the wool tree cutout. Place the cutout, face down, on a flat work surface and align the stabilizer pattern over it as shown.

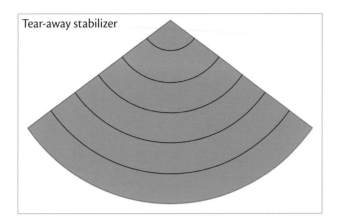

Tear-away stabilizer

2. Straight stitch directly on the garland placement lines, and then flip the piece right side up. Starting from the top of the tree, directly on the first arched line, sew one of your favorite decorative stitches, using the line of straight stitching as a guide. Sew another decorative stitch (either the same or different) on the third and fifth garland placement lines.

3. On the second and fourth garland placement lines, sew a row of rickrack. Align the bottom row of rickrack with the bottom edge of the wool.

4. Remove the stabilizer and trim any excess rickrack. Set aside.

5. Apply a ¼"-wide strip of fusible-web tape to one side of the pom-pom fringe heading. *Do not* remove the paper backing at this time. Remove the paper backing from the felt lining. Finger-press the untreated side of the pom-pom heading to the bottom edge of the wrong side of the felt lining. Fuse, following the manufacturer's instructions and using a Teflon pressing sheet to protect the iron and ironing surface.

6. Remove the paper backing from the pom-pom fringe. Layer the wool with the decorative garlands on top of the felt lining, matching all edges and smoothing out all wrinkles. The pom-pom fringe is now sandwiched between the felt lining and the wool. Fuse.

7. Sew the buttons to the right side of the tree slipcover between the garland lines as shown.

8. Fold the tree slipcover in half, wrong sides together, aligning the unfinished edges. Pin. Sew the back seam of the slipcover using a ¼" seam allowance.

TREE ASSEMBLY

1. On the wooden dowel, mark a point 3" from the top and a point 8" from the bottom. Paint the center section of the dowel brown. Let dry.

2. Starting at the 3" mark, hot glue the 12"-long cinnamon sticks to the painted area of the dowel. Cover any gaps by gluing on leftover cinnamon sticks cut to size.

3. Fill a mixing bowl with dry floral foam. Insert the 8" unpainted portion of the dowel into the center of the foam and push the dowel down to the bottom of the bowl. Mark the center point on the bottom of the craft cone and slide the cone straight down onto the dowel, stopping at the cinnamon sticks. *Tip: Pinch the top of the craft cone with your fingers to make a nice point.*

4. Completely cover the floral foam in the basket with the red berries and evergreen sprigs.

5. Place the tree slipcover onto the craft cone.

Sugar Cookie Christmas Tree

What could be more fun than "planting" a Sugar Cookie Christmas Tree in your kitchen? Add some cinnamon sticks and a mixing bowl filled with faux snow, berries, or vintage-looking cookie cutters, and you have an eye-catching kitchen decoration for the holidays. This charming display piece, complete with brilliant red Swirl Ball Sugar Cookie Ornaments, is sure to become a holiday classic.

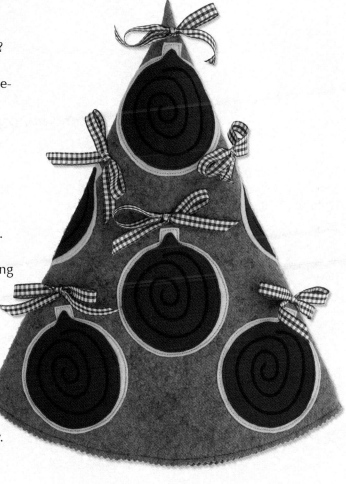

This tree is an easy variation of the Gingerbread Cookie Dough Tree on page 41. Both the slipcover and lining are made from relish green wool felt. Fuse the front and lining together and then, for a decorative touch, stitch ¼" from the lower edge and trim close to the edge using pinking shears or a rotary cutter with a pinking blade.

In place of the garlands, buttons, and pom-pom fringe, stitch eight Swirl Ball ornament fronts (see Sugar Cookie Ornaments on page 7) to the slipcover and embellish each with a red gingham bow. As a finishing touch once the tree is assembled, tie a ½-yard length of ⅝"-wide wired gingham ribbon in a bow around the center of the cinnamon-stick tree trunk.

43

Cooling Cookies WALL HANGING

Use this festive quilted wall hanging, with scrumptious sugar cookie appliqués, as a focal point in an entry or above a buffet table. It could also become a whimsical table covering for a side table.

FINISHED SIZE: 35½" X 35½"

INGREDIENTS

Yields 1 wall hanging.

2 yards of black-and-white check fabric for cooling racks and backing

1⅛ yards of prequilted white fabric for quilt top

⅓ yard of black fabric with white polka dots for binding

⅛ yard of black wool felt

39" x 39" square of cotton batting

¼ yard of fusible web, 18" wide

7 yards (3 packages) of jumbo (¾"-wide) black rickrack

Embroidery thread

Thread for construction

Seam sealant

Fine-tipped permanent marker

Freezer paper

Temporary spray adhesive

For Sugar Cookie Ornaments:

⅝ yard of buttercream wool felt for backgrounds

¼ yard of bright red wool felt for icing

6" x 9" rectangle *each* of lemon, light green, white, baby blue, and peacock wool felt for icing

Scrap of orange wool felt for Snowman's nose

1 skein of chocolate brown cotton floss (DMC #898) for Snowman's eyes

CUTTING

From the black-and-white check fabric, cut:
1 square, 39" x 39"

5 squares, 11" x 11"

From the prequilted white fabric, cut:
1 square, 36" x 36"

From the black fabric with white polka dots, cut:
4 strips, 2½" x width of fabric

SUGAR COOKIE RECIPE

Prepare 13 Sugar Cookie Ornaments (fronts only) using the instructions on pages 7–8 as a guide. Make five Swirl Balls, two Snowmen, two Christmas Trees, two Bells, and two Stars. Set aside.

BACKING, BATTING, AND QUILTING

1. Lay the quilt backing, wrong side up, on a flat work surface and spray with spray adhesive. Layer the cotton batting on top of the backing, matching all the edges, and smooth out any wrinkles.

2. Spray the back of the prequilted quilt top with spray adhesive and center, right side up, on top of the batting and backing layers. The batting and backing will be 1½" larger than the quilt top on all sides.

COOLING-RACK ASSEMBLY

1. Find the horizontal and vertical center of the quilt top. Mark by finger-pressing.

2. Apply spray adhesive to the back of an 11" checked square (cooling rack square). Position the square on point at the center of the quilt top, aligning the points of the square with the finger-pressed lines from step 1.

3. Apply spray adhesive to the back of the four remaining 11" checked squares. Place one square in each of the four corners, 2" from the cut edges on each side.

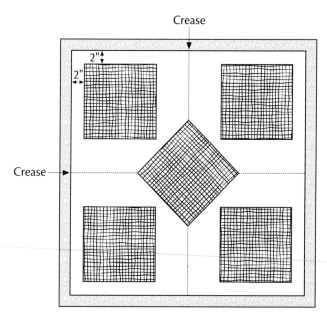

Crease

Crease

2"

2"

4. Quilt the cooling rack squares to the quilt top using your favorite method.

5. Starting with the center square, sew rickrack around the perimeter of the square. When approaching the end, stop sewing with the needle in the "down" position on the rickrack. Determine how much more rickrack you'll need to complete the square, trim the rickrack ¼" beyond what is needed, apply seam sealant to the cut end, and turn under ¼". Then, continue sewing the rickrack down and backstitch. Repeat for the remaining cooling rack squares.

6. Trim the excess batting and backing even with the edges of the quilt top.

ADDING APPLIQUÉS

1. Apply fusible web to the back of the black felt, following the manufacturer's directions. Do *not* remove the paper backing at this time. Using the marker, trace one *each* of the "COOLING COOKIES" letters and two stars onto the *un-coated* side of the freezer paper, using the patterns on page 84. Cut on the marked lines.

2. Using a *dry* iron, press the freezer-paper patterns, *shiny* side down, onto the right side of the black felt. Cut out the letters and stars.

3. Remove the paper backing from the letters and stars. Position them onto the center square, allowing sufficient room in the center for the sugar cookie placement. Fuse, and then stitch the letters and stars in place, close to the cut edges.

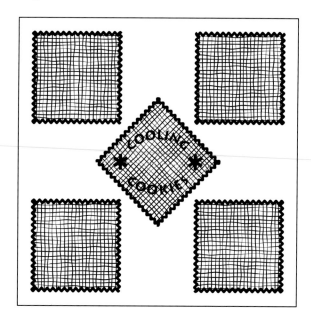

4. Apply spray adhesive to the back of each sugar cookie front. Arrange the cookies on the cooling racks as shown, and stitch in place close to the cut edges.

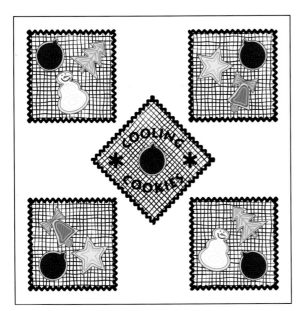

ADDING THE BINDING

1. Fold the binding strips in half lengthwise, wrong sides together. Press.

2. Align the raw edges of one binding strip with the side edge of the quilt top. Pin and then sew in place. Repeat on the opposite side. Press the binding strips away from the quilt top and trim the excess.

3. Repeat step 2 for the top and bottom edges of the quilt top.

4. Fold the side binding strips to the back of the quilt so that the edge of the binding meets the stitching line, and pin in place. Repeat for the top and bottom binding strips. Whipstitch the binding to the quilt back.

Cooling Cookies Pillow

This 20" pillow can be used to continue the "cooling cookies" theme throughout a room. Use it to accessorize a couch, a favorite chair, or a child's bed. The pillows make the perfect cushions for children or grandchildren to use when lying on the floor to watch the holiday shows. For a special touch, put each child's favorite cookies on the pillow, so they know which one is theirs.

Using the instructions for the Cooling Cookies Wall Hanging on pages 45–47 as a guide, you can make this pillow easily. Start with two 21" squares of prequilted white fabric and embellish the center of one with the cooling cookies rack (on point), rickrack trim, and Sugar Cookie Ornaments. Add pom-pom fringe to the outer edge and then stitch the pillow front to the back around the outer edges, leaving an opening for turning. Turn right side out, insert a pillow form, and slipstitch the opening closed.

Small Sugar Cookie STOCKING

For deliciously unique place settings, use a bright red stocking as a
utensil holder in combination with the ivory Holly Button Plate Charger/Place Mat
on page 15 or make the stocking in green to go with the red
Holly Button Tray/Place Mat on page 19.

FINISHED SIZE: APPROXIMATELY 7" X 10"

INGREDIENTS

Yields 1 stocking.

12" x 18" rectangle of buttercream wool felt for
background

2½" x 5" rectangle of white wool felt for cuff icing

7" x 9" rectangle of bright red wool felt for stocking
icing

⅞ yard of red-and-white checked ribbon,
⅜" wide

⅜ yard of tear-away stabilizer,
20" wide

Embroidery thread to coordinate or
contrast with each icing color and
for piped icing

Seam sealant

Fine-tipped permanent marker

Freezer paper

Temporary spray adhesive

Teflon pressing sheet

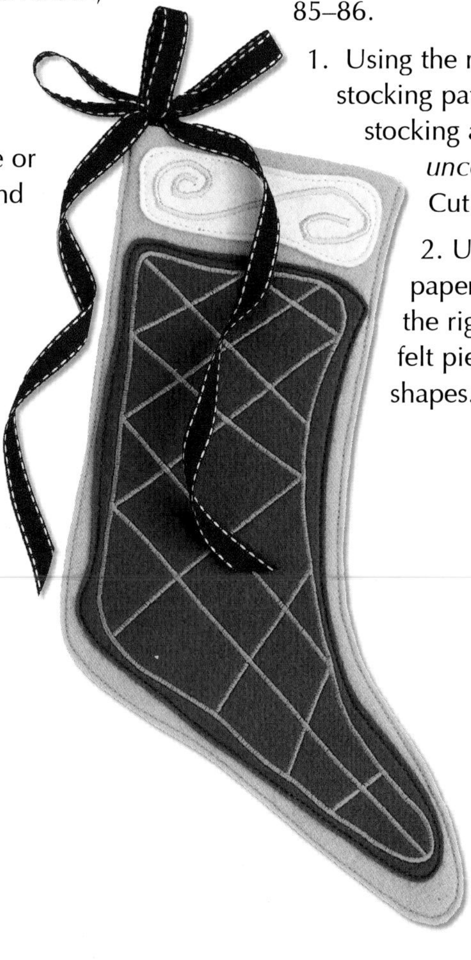

CUTTING

From the red-and-white checked ribbon, cut:
1 piece, 4½" long, for hanging loop
1 piece, 24" long, for bow

PATTERN PREPARATION

The following instructions are for one small
Christmas stocking. Use the patterns on pages
85–86.

1. Using the marker, trace the outer line of the
    stocking pattern, the reverse image, and the
    stocking and cuff icing patterns onto the
    uncoated side of the freezer paper.
    Cut on the marked lines.

2. Using a *dry* iron, press the freezer-
    paper patterns, *shiny* side down, onto
    the right side of the corresponding wool
    felt pieces. Cut out the stocking and icing
    shapes. Set aside.

PIPED-ICING PREPARATION

1. Cut a piece of tear-away stabilizer larger than both of the icing cutouts. Trace the icing designs and dashed placement lines onto the stabilizer, using the icing guide provided with the stocking pattern. *Note that the icing patterns are reversed.*

2. Lightly apply spray adhesive to the back of the stabilizer pattern. Adhere the stabilizer to the back of the icing cutouts, aligning the dashed lines with the outer edges of the cutouts. Straight stitch along all piped icing design lines.

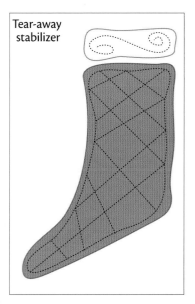

3. Flip the icing over so that the front side faces up. Satin stitch directly on top of the straight-stitched lines. Pull the thread tails to the back side. Knot and trim the excess thread. Remove the excess stabilizer.

STOCKING ASSEMBLY

1. Lightly apply spray adhesive to the back of the icing pieces and center the icing pieces, right side up, onto a buttercream stocking piece. Using a straight stitch, sew close to the edges of the icing pieces.

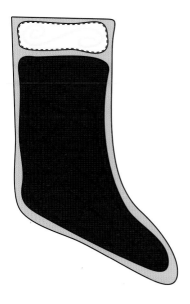

2. Pin the stocking front to the back, wrong sides together, matching all edges.

3. Fold the 4½"-long piece of checked ribbon for the hanging loop in half and sandwich the ribbon ½" down between the stocking front and back pieces. Hand sew the ribbon to the inside stocking back, aligning it with the side edge.

4. Stitch close to the cut edges of the stocking pieces, leaving the top edge open and making sure to catch the hanging-loop ribbon in the seam.

5. Cut the ends of the 24"-long checked ribbon at an angle and apply seam sealant to the cut edges. Tie the ribbon into a bow. Tack or hot glue the knot of the bow onto the small hanging loop where it meets at the top edge of the stocking.

Gingerbread STOCKING

You can almost smell the aroma of freshly baked gingerbread when you feast your eyes on this cookie-inspired stocking. Complete the look by adding a bow that looks like peppermint ribbon candy cascading down the back. This large stocking is designed to be hung in a traditional manner on a mantelpiece or door and filled with treats and surprises or holiday greenery.

FINISHED SIZE: APPROXIMATELY 10" X 16"

INGREDIENTS

Yields 1 stocking.

1 fat quarter of gingerbread-colored wool for stocking

⅓ yard of white wool felt for lining

1½ yards of red-and-white striped grosgrain ribbon, ⅝" wide

2 yards (1 package) of white jumbo (¾"-wide) rickrack

⅝ yard of fusible web, 18" wide

½ yard of tear-away stabilizer, 20" wide

Embroidery thread for piped icing

Seam sealant

Fine-tipped permanent marker

Freezer paper

Temporary spray adhesive

Teflon pressing sheet

CUTTING

From the rickrack, cut:
1 piece, 8" long, for hanging loop

PATTERN PREPARATION

1. Apply fusible web to the back of the gingerbread-colored wool, following the manufacturer's directions. *Do not* remove the paper backing at this time.

2. Using the marker, trace the outline for the stocking pattern (page 87) and the reverse image onto the *uncoated* side of freezer paper. Cut on the marked lines.

3. Using a *dry* iron, press the freezer-paper patterns, *shiny* side down, onto the right side of the wool. Cut on the marked lines. Remove the pattern and iron it *shiny* side down onto the right side of the white felt. Cut out the stocking shapes.

PIPED ICING AND RICKRACK

1. Cut a piece of tear-away stabilizer larger than the stocking cutout. Using the piped icing guide provided with the pattern, trace the dashed placement line and the piped icing design onto the piece of stabilizer. *Note that the piped icing patterns are reversed.*

2. Remove the paper backing from the stocking front piece only. Adhere the tear-away stabilizer to the back of the stocking front, lining up the outside pattern lines with the outer edges of

the stocking. *Do not iron* the stabilizer to the cutout. Straight stitch along all icing design lines.

3. Flip the stocking right side up and satin stitch directly on top of the straight-stitched icing lines. Remove the excess stabilizer.

4. Remove the paper backing from the stocking back piece. Pin the rickrack to the back of the stocking front around all edges, and also to the back of the stocking back piece along only the upper edge as shown.

5. Place the stocking cutouts, right side up, on a pressing sheet and fuse the rickrack and thread tails to the back of the cutout. Let cool completely and then lift the cutouts from the pressing sheet. Cut away excess thread tails and remove the pins. This process fuses the thread tails to the back of the stocking front to avoid raveling and fuses the rickrack in place.

STOCKING ASSEMBLY

1. Fold the 8" length of rickrack in half. Lap the cut ends ½" over the top edge of the lining for the stocking back as shown and pin.

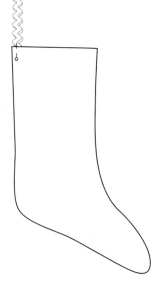

2. Layer the stocking front and back pieces over the lining pieces, aligning all edges and taking care to sandwich the rickrack between the lining and stocking pieces. Fuse.

3. Straight stitch through all layers ⅛" from the top of the stocking front and back. I used a double straight stitch (a decorative stitch) to keep the stitches from sinking into the fabric.

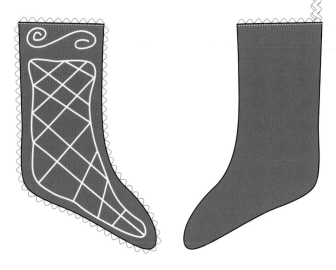

4. Pin the stocking front to the back, with the lining sides together. Straight stitch around the stocking ⅛" from the edges (I used a double straight stitch), leaving the top edge unstitched.

5. From the length of grosgrain ribbon, make a bow and tack or hot glue the knot of the bow to the base of the rickrack hanging loop. Trim the ribbon ends at an angle and apply seam sealant to the cut edges.

6. If desired, tack or glue the ribbon tails in a swirl along the back edge of the stocking.

Ginger Cookie
PUNCHNEEDLE ORNAMENTS

Let it snow! Let it snow! Let it snow! Snowflakes will be everywhere
once you get started on these fast, fun, and easy Russian punchneedle ornaments.
Backed with wool felt, these little treasures are the perfect take-along projects.
Before you know it, you'll be in a blizzard of ginger cookie snowflakes!

FINISHED SIZE: 5" X 5"

INGREDIENTS

Yields 3 ornaments. Skein requirements for cotton floss can vary, as everyone punches differently and floss brands differ. This means that the loop length and punching density are unique. The skein amounts listed below reflect what I used to complete the three punchneedle ornaments.

⅓ yard of weaver's cloth

¼ yard of Norwegian blue wool felt

⅓ yard of heavyweight stiff interfacing, 13" wide

DMC cotton embroidery floss:

- 6 skeins of medium brown (DMC #433) for ginger cookies (2 skeins per ornament)
- 6 skeins of light lavender blue (DMC #3840) for background (2 skeins per ornament)
- 1 skein of white (DMC blanc) for piped snow-flake pattern

1½ yards of brown-and-white polka-dot ribbon, ⅜" wide

1½ yards of brown-and-white dashed-line ribbon, ⅛" wide

1½ yards of brown-and-white check ribbon, ¼" wide

¾ yard of brown-and-white stitched-edge grosgrain ribbon, ⅜" wide

Seam sealant

Fine-tipped permanent marker

Freezer paper

Scallop-edged scissors or rotary cutter with a scallop blade

7" x 7" gripper frame or a 7" locking hoop

3-strand punchneedle

Very sharp, small scissors

Clear fabric glue

Hot-glue gun and glue sticks

CUTTING

From the weaver's cloth, cut:
3 squares, 11" x 11"

From the brown-and-white polka-dot ribbon, cut:
3 pieces, 18" long; cut the ends at an angle and apply seam sealant to the cut edges

From the brown-and-white dashed-line ribbon, cut:
3 pieces, 18" long; cut the ends at an angle and

apply seam sealant to the cut edges

From the brown-and-white check ribbon, cut:
3 pieces, 18" long; cut the ends at an angle and apply seam sealant to the cut edges

From the brown-and-white double-dashed-line grosgrain ribbon, cut:
3 pieces, 4½" long

PATTERN PREPARATION

Please read all directions before beginning this project.

1. Using the marker and the patterns on pages 88–89, trace the *inner* hexagon line for one snowflake ornament onto the *uncoated* side of the freezer paper. Cut on the marked line. Set aside.

2. Trace the *outer* hexagon line for one ornament onto the *uncoated* side of the freezer paper, leaving at least ½" of space around the outline. Then, using scallop-edged scissors or a scallop rotary blade, begin cutting on the marked line so that the inside edge of the scallop meets with the outside edge of the marked line.

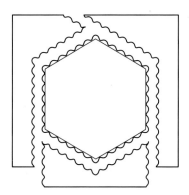

3. Using a *dry* iron, press the small freezer-paper hexagon pattern, *shiny* side down, onto the right side of the heavyweight stiff interfacing and press the scallop-edged freezer-paper hexagon, *shiny* side down, onto the blue felt.

4. For the heavyweight interfacing, cut along the outer edge of the pattern. To ensure that the felt backing for each ornament looks the same, line up the scallop blade with the freezer-paper scallop pattern and cut out the ornament backings. Remove the patterns and reuse them to cut two more hexagons from interfacing and two more scallop-edged hexagons from felt for the remaining ornaments.

PREPARING THE WEAVER'S CLOTH

You'll notice that the weaver's cloth stretches in one direction but not the other. Place the design on the fabric so that the fabric stretches from top to bottom.

1. Place the pattern under the square of weaver's cloth and use the marker to trace all but the outer hexagon line.

2. For punching ease, secure the weaver's cloth very tightly in a gripper frame or locking hoop without distorting the design. Straighten the design as you tighten the fabric in the frame or hoop.

PUNCHING THE SNOWFLAKES

Repeat the recipe for each ornament. Refer to your punchneedle instruction booklet for proper use and needle threading. This punchneedle embroidery design was made using a three-strand punchneedle that was set to produce loops ¼" long. The embroidery floss should be able to move through the needle freely, so adjust the floss as needed.

1. Using white floss, punch directly on the snowflake lines, once for a very thin snowflake and twice for a thicker snowflake. The snowflakes I made were punched twice.

2. Using medium brown floss, punch just inside the outline for the cookie shape and then fill it in with color close to the punched snowflake.

3. For a seamless appearance, punch around the gingerbread shape using light lavender blue floss. Outline the hexagon shape and continue punching until the background meets the outline around the gingerbread cookie. Fill in any remaining spaces.

4. Before removing the punched ornament from your frame or hoop, turn the design right side up and check to make sure that all areas are punched and that there are no gaps. Fill in any gaps as needed, and then remove the design from your frame or hoop.

FINISHING

1. For a uniform apperance, use very sharp scissors to carefully trim any long or loose pieces of floss to the same length as the punched loops. Trim the beginning and ending thread tails in the same manner.

2. Trim the excess weaver's cloth, leaving about ½" around the punched design. If needed, place the punched design right side down on a fluffy terrycloth towel and lightly press the back of the design flat, being careful not to smash the punched loops.

3. Lay the punched design, wrong side up, on a flat work surface. Center and place the heavyweight interfacing hexagon directly on top of the punched hexagon, matching all edges. If needed, trim the interfacing hexagon to size.

4. At each point of the hexagon, cut the weaver's cloth at an angle to within ⅛" to ¼" of the interfacing cutout. You now have six flaps.

5. Apply clear fabric glue just inside the perimeter of the interfacing hexagon and fold the flaps over the glue and onto the back of the interfacing, making sure the glue holds the flaps snugly in place. Let dry completely. If desired, use a permanent marker the same color as the background loops and carefully "color" the exposed weaver's cloth.

6. To make the hanging loop, fold a 4½" length of grosgrain ribbon in half. Place the cut ends of the ribbon on the back of the ornament front, ½" from the top point. Hand sew the ribbon onto the back of the interfacing.

7. Turn the punched ornament front face down on a flat work surface. Apply clear fabric glue to the back and then center and adhere the punched ornament front to the blue felt ornament backing. The hanging loop is now sandwiched between the ornament front and back.

8. Tie the three coordinating 18" lengths of ribbon into a single bow. Center a dot of hot glue on the hanging loop, where the wool felt backing comes to a point, and adhere the back of the bow knot to the hanging loop.

Sugar Cookie
PUNCHNEEDLE ORNAMENTS

Trimming the Christmas tree has never been so much fun.
Quickly punch a Holiday Bell, a Christmas Pine, and a Sugar Cookie of the Year
to add a festive touch to your home for the holiday season.

FINISHED SIZE OF OVAL HOLIDAY BELL AND CHRISTMAS PINE: 4½" X 5½"
FINISHED SIZE OF ROUND SUGAR COOKIE OF THE YEAR: 4½" X 4½"

INGREDIENTS

Yields 3 ornaments: a Holiday Bell, Christmas Pine, and Sugar Cookie of the Year. Skein requirements for cotton floss can vary, as everyone punches differently and floss brands differ. This means that the loop length and punching density are unique. The skein amounts listed below reflect what I used to complete the three punchneedle ornaments.

⅓ yard of weaver's cloth

1 fat quarter of green herringbone wool for backgrounds of Holiday Bell and Christmas Pine

1 square, 6" x 6", of buttercream wool felt for Sugar Cookie of the Year background

¼ yard of heavyweight stiff interfacing, 13" wide

DMC cotton embroidery floss (for Holiday Bell and Christmas Pine):

- 6 skeins of off-white (DMC ecru) for background (3 skeins for each ornament)
- 2 skeins of light green (DMC #164) for tree icing
- 1 skein of dark forest green (DMC #986) for pine garland stems
- 1 skein of medium forest green (DMC #988) for pine needles

- 1 skein of light tan (DMC #738) for cookie backgrounds
- 1 skein of medium kelly green (DMC #702) for piped icing tree branches
- 1 skein of dark turquoise (DMC #3810) for bell icing, bow piped icing, and bell hammer piped icing
- 1 skein of light turquoise (DMC #3811) for bow icing, bell hammer icing, and bell piped icing

DMC cotton embroidery floss (for Sugar Cookie of the Year):

- 3 skeins of pistachio green (DMC #369) for icing
- 2 skeins of medium tan (DMC #437) for cookie background
- 1 skein of white (DMC blanc) for icing swirls
- 1 skein of dark coral red (DMC #817) for date

6 red Ken buttons, ¼" diameter, for Holiday Bell and Christmas Pine, 3 per ornament (Just Another Button Company)

2 large red peppermint buttons for Sugar Cookie of the Year (Just Another Button Company)

1⅛ yards of red-and-white check ribbon, ⅜" wide, for Holiday Bell and Christmas Pine

(Ingredients continued on page 60)

(Ingredients continued from page 59)

²/₃ yard of red-and-white striped grosgrain ribbon,
⁵/₈" wide, for Sugar Cookie of the Year

Seam sealant

Fine-tipped permanent marker

Freezer paper

Scallop-edged scissors or rotary cutter with a scallop
blade

7" x 7" gripper frame or a 7" locking hoop

3-strand punchneedle

Very sharp, small scissors

Clear fabric glue

Hot-glue gun and glue sticks

CUTTING

From the weaver's cloth, cut:
3 squares, 11" x 11"

From the red-and-white check ribbon, cut:
2 pieces, 13½" long; trim the ends at an angle and
apply seam sealant to the cut edges

2 pieces, 4½" long

From the ⁵/₈" red-and-white striped ribbon, cut:
1 piece, 18" long; cut the ends into a dovetail
(V shape) and apply seam sealant to the cut edges

1 piece, 5" long

PATTERN PREPARATION

Please read all directions before beginning this
project.

1. Using the marker and the ornament patterns
   on pages 89–90, trace the inner circle of the
   Sugar Cookie of the Year ornament and the
   oval pattern outline for the Holiday Bell and
   Christmas Pine ornaments onto the *uncoated*
   side of freezer paper. Cut on the marked lines.

2. Using a *dry* iron, press the freezer-paper
   patterns, *shiny* side down, onto the right side of
   the heavyweight stiff interfacing. Cut around the
   outer edges of the patterns. Set aside.

3. Trace the outer line of the Sugar Cookie of the
   Year ornament onto the *uncoated* side of the
   freezer paper, leaving at least ½" beyond the
   drawn line. To make the pattern for the backing of the oval ornaments, draw a 4½" x 5½"
   rectangle onto the *uncoated* side of the freezer
   paper, leaving at least ½" beyond the drawn
   lines. Then, using scallop-edged scissors or a
   scallop rotary blade, cut out the shapes so that
   the inside edge of the scallop meets with the
   outside edge of the marked lines as shown.

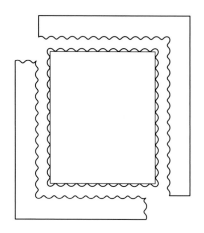

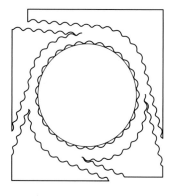

4. Using a *dry* iron, press the scallop-edged
   patterns, *shiny* side down, onto the right side
   of the appropriate color of wool or wool felt.
   To ensure that the backing for each ornament
   looks the same, line up the scallop blade with
   the freezer-paper scallop pattern and cut out
   the ornament backings. Remove the patterns.
   Reuse the rectangle pattern to cut one more
   ornament back piece for the remaining oval
   ornament.

PREPARING THE WEAVER'S CLOTH

You'll notice that the weaver's cloth stretches in one direction but not the other. Place the design on the fabric so that the fabric stretches from top to bottom.

1. Place the pattern for one of the three ornaments under the square of weaver's cloth. Use the marker to trace the design onto the weaver's cloth. Change the year for the Sugar Cookie of the Year ornament, if desired, using the numbers provided on page 89.

2. Using the pattern as a placement guide, position the buttons (red berries for the oval ornaments and peppermint buttons for the round ornament) on the weaver's cloth and carefully trace around the perimeter of each button. Handmade buttons vary in size, so it's important to note which button goes where. Set the buttons aside after tracing them.

3. For punching ease, secure the weaver's cloth very tightly in a gripper frame or a locking hoop without distorting the design. Straighten the design as you tighten the fabric in the frame or hoop.

PUNCHING THE ORNAMENTS

Refer to your punchneedle instruction booklet for proper use and needle threading. This punchneedle embroidery design was made using a three-strand punchneedle that was set to produce loops ¼" long. The embroidery floss should be able to move through the needle freely, so adjust the floss as needed.

1. **Christmas Pine.** Punch directly on the pattern lines for the pine garland stem with dark forest green and then the pine needles with medium forest green. Punch the piped icing tree branches using medium kelly green. Outline the piped icing branches and the tree icing with light green; then fill in until the tree icing area is covered. Punch around the icing with light tan and then outline the sugar cookie tree. Continue punching until the sugar cookie area is filled in.

Punch the background with ecru, outlining the garland stem, the needles, and the sugar cookie tree itself and then punching around the button markings and the ornament outline. Fill in until the background is completely covered, except for the button openings.

Holiday Bell. Punch directly on the pattern lines for the pine garland stem with dark forest green and then the pine needles with medium forest green. Punch the piped icing lines for the bell with light turquoise and the piped icing lines for the bow and bell hammer with dark turquoise. Outline the piped icing lines and the icing outline for the bell with dark turquoise and then fill the area in. Outline the piped icing lines and the icing outline for the bow and bell hammer with light turquoise and then fill the area in. Punch around the icing with light tan and then outline the sugar cookie bell. Continue punching until the sugar cookie bell area is filled in.

Punch the background with ecru, outlining the garland stem and needles and the sugar cookie bell itself and then punching around the button markings and the ornament outline. Fill in until the background is completely covered, except for the button openings.

Sugar Cookie of the Year. Punch directly on the pattern lines for the icing swirls using white floss. Punch on the outline of the year and fill in with dark coral red. Punch with pistachio green around the shapes created above, around the button outlines, and on the icing outline. Continue punching until the icing area is filled in, except for the button openings. Punch around the icing with medium tan for the background and punch around the sugar cookie outline. Continue filling in the sugar cookie background until the area is filled in.

2. Before removing the punched ornament from your frame or hoop, turn the design right side up and check to make sure that all areas are punched and that there are no gaps. Fill in any gaps as needed, and then remove the design from your frame or hoop.

FINISHING

1. For a uniform appearance, use very sharp scissors to carefully trim any long or loose pieces of floss to the same length as the punched loops. Trim the beginning and ending thread tails in the same manner.

2. Position the buttons snugly into place flat against the weaver's cloth, making sure that no loops are underneath the buttons. Sew the buttons in place with the needle and thread. Trim the excess weaver's cloth, leaving about 1" around the punched design.

3. If needed, place the punched design right side down on a fluffy terrycloth towel and lightly press the back of the design flat, being careful not to smash the punched loops.

4. Lay the punched design, wrong side up, on a flat work surface. Make several cuts around the weaver's cloth to within 1/8" to 1/4" of the center. The more cuts you make, the better your shape will be. You now have lots of small flaps.

5. Center and place the oval or circle cut from heavyweight stiff interfacing on the back of the corresponding punched design, matching all edges. If needed, trim the interfacing shapes to size.

6. Apply clear fabric glue to the back, just inside the perimeter of the interfacing cutout. Fold the flaps over the glue and onto the back of the interfacing cutout, making sure the glue holds the flaps snugly in place. The flaps will overlap one another. Let dry completely. If desired,

use a permanent marker the same color as the background loops and carefully "color" the exposed weaver's cloth.

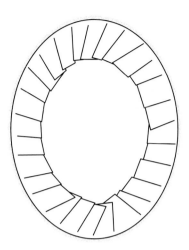

7. To make the hanging loop for the oval ornaments, fold the 4½" lengths of check ribbon in half. For the round ornament, fold the 5" length of striped ribbon in half. Place the cut end of the ribbon on the back of the ornament front, ½" from the top of the ornament. Hand sew the ribbon to the back of the interfacing.

8. Place the ornament front right side down on a flat work surface. Apply clear fabric glue to the back, and then center and stick the punched ornament front to the wool rectangle or the wool felt circle for the ornament backing. The hanging loop is now sandwiched between the ornament front and back.

9. For the oval ornaments, tie the 13½"-long ribbons into bows. For the round ornament, tie the 18"-long ribbon into a bow. Center a dot of hot glue on the hanging loop where the wool or wool felt backing begins, and adhere the back of the bow knot to the hanging loop.

Ginger Cookie LINED APRON

Declare your "baking artistry" with this stylish full apron that will protect
your clothing while you fly around the kitchen whipping up batches of cookie dough!
Three large pockets keep utensils and favorite cookie recipes close at hand.
Adjustable ribbon neck and waist ties ensure a perfect fit.

FINISHED SIZE: APPROXIMATELY 22" X 31"

INGREDIENTS

*Yields 1 apron. Use only prewashed and colorfast
fabrics, wool felt, and wools for the apron.*

2 yards of green-and-ivory check cotton fabric for
apron and apron lining

½ yard of ivory tonal cotton print for apron patch
and pocket

⅜ yard of brown cotton fabric for apron patch
background

1 fat quarter of gingerbread-colored wool for snowflake cookies on apron pockets

⅜ yard of fusible web, 18" wide

½ yard of tear-away stabilizer, 20" wide

1½ yards of fusible-web tape, ¼" wide

White embroidery thread for piped icing

Thread for construction

1 skein of gingerbread brown (DMC #898) cotton
floss

7 yards of hunter green stitched-edge grosgrain
ribbon, ⅝" wide

3 yards of green rickrack, ⅜" wide

Seam sealant

Ultrafine-tipped permanent marker

Freezer paper

Embroidery hoop

Removable fabric marker

Acrylic ruler

Rotary cutter

6 peppermint swirl buttons (Just Another Button
Company): 2 small and 4 medium

1 medium holly sprig button (Just Another Button
Company)

CUTTING

From the green-and-ivory check cotton fabric, cut:
2 rectangles, 23" x 32"

From the ivory tonal cotton print, cut:
1 rectangle, 14½" x 15½"
1 square, 11" x 11"

From the brown cotton fabric, cut:
1 rectangle, 15" x 8½"
1 rectangle, 5" x 9"

From the green ribbon, cut:
2 pieces, 54" long, for waist ribbons; cut an angle
on one end of each ribbon and apply seam sealant to the cut edges

2 pieces, 36" long, for neck ribbons; cut an angle
on one end of each ribbon and apply seam sealant to the cut edges

3 pieces, 18" long, for bows on pockets; cut a
dovetail (V shape) on both ends of each ribbon
and apply seam sealant to the cut edges

From the fusible web, cut:
1 rectangle, 5" x 9"

GINGER COOKIE RECIPE

Prepare three Ginger Cookie Snowflake Ornaments (fronts only) using the instructions for "Pattern Preparation" and "Piped Icing" on pages 11–12 as a guide. Make one of each snowflake style. Set aside.

MAKING THE PATCH

1. Trace the outer edge of the apron patch pattern on page 91 onto the paper side of the 5" x 9" piece of fusible web. Apply the fusible web to the back of the 5" x 9" brown fabric rectangle, following the manufacturer's directions. Cut out the oval background. *Do not* remove the backing paper. Set aside.

2. Place the "Baking Artist" pattern, right side up, under the ivory tonal fabric square. Using a light box or sunny window, trace the words with the permanent marker. Trace the inner oval line just outside the pattern line, so that when it is cut away the line will not be seen in the final buttonhole stitching process.

3. Place the patch fabric in an embroidery hoop. Using three strands of cotton floss, backstitch directly over the traced letters drawn in step 2. Use a French knot to dot the "i." Remove the fabric from the hoop and press carefully.

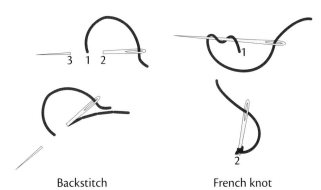

Backstitch   French knot

4. Apply fusible web to the back of the ivory fabric square. Cut just inside the marked oval line and remove the paper backing.

5. Center the "Baking Artist" patch on the brown background oval (which still has the paper backing attached) and carefully fuse. Stitch

around the raw edge of the lettered oval using a machine buttonhole stitch. Set aside.

POCKET PREPARATION

1. Fold the ivory rectangle, wrong sides together, to create a 14½" x 7¾" rectangle. Finger-press to identify where the eventual top of the pockets will be.

2. Open the rectangle, right side facing up. Use a removable fabric marker to draw a line 5" from the left side, extending from the finger-pressed fold line to the bottom cut edge. Repeat on the right side of the rectangle.

3. Run a basting stitch along the lines drawn in step 2, and then completely remove the fabric marker lines following the manufacturer's directions.

4. Center the three ginger cookie snowflake fronts between the basting lines, 2" from the bottom cut edge of the pocket, and fuse the cookies in place following the manufacturer's directions.

5. Place a piece of tear-away stabilizer, cut larger than the stitching area, under the snowflakes. Use a narrow zigzag stitch to stitch around all edges of each snowflake. Remove the stabilizer.

6. Fold the ivory rectangle, right sides together, to again create a 14½" x 7¾" rectangle. Sew ¼" from the cut edges, leaving a 3" to 4" opening at the bottom.

7. Trim the corners close to the stitching and turn the rectangle right side out. At the opening, turn the seam allowance in ¼" and press the entire rectangle. Set aside.

8. Apply ¼"–wide fusible-web tape to the back of the brown rectangle, matching the edge of the tape to the cut edge of the fabric. Set aside.

APRON ASSEMBLY

1. Using the rectangle for the apron front, mark 20" from the bottom on opposite sides. At the top, mark 7" from the left and right edges.

2. Fold the rectangle in half lengthwise, matching the edges and markings. Align an acrylic ruler with the 7" and 20" marks, and then cut along the ruler with a rotary cutter. Cut the apron lining to match the apron front.

3. Remove the paper backing from the brown oval; then center the "Baking Artist" patch 2½" from the top of the apron front. Fuse in place. Put a piece of tear-away stabilizer, larger than the patch, underneath the apron front. Machine buttonhole stitch around the perimeter of the oval.

4. Sew peppermint and holly buttons in place, using the pattern as a placement guide.

5. Remove the paper strips from the brown pocket backing. Center and fuse the backing to the apron front, 6" from the bottom of the apron.

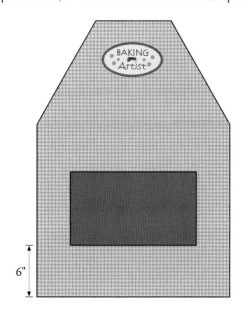

6. Put a piece of tear-away stabilizer, larger than the pocket backing, underneath the pocket area of the apron front. Machine buttonhole stitch around the perimeter of the pocket backing.

7. Center and pin the ivory rectangle onto the brown pocket backing. Approximately ½" of the brown rectangle should show all around. Stitch ⅛" from the side and bottom edges.

8. Using the basting stitches as a guide, straight stitch from the top of the ivory pocket to the bottom. Repeat along the second basting line. Remove the basting stitches. You now have three pockets on the apron.

9. Align an end of each waist ribbon with an edge of the apron front, ½" from the angled corners. Pin the ribbons and then baste them in place. Align, pin, and then baste the neck ribbons to top of the apron front, ½" from the angled corners. Tuck the unpinned ribbon ends into the apron pockets to avoid catching them when sewing the final seams.

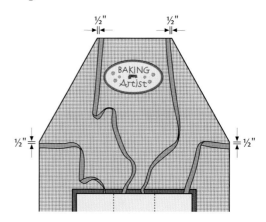

10. Place the apron right side up on a flat surface. Stack the lining face down on the apron front, matching all edges, and pin the lining to the apron.

11. Stitch ½" from the edges, leaving a 4" to 5" opening at the bottom. Trim corners close to the stitching and turn the apron right side out.

12. At the opening, turn the seam allowance under ½". Press the entire apron, being careful not to touch the buttons with the hot iron.

FINISHING

1. Using an acrylic ruler as a guide, mark a line ½" from the finished edges of the apron. Pin rickrack over the line and then stitch in place.

2. Make three bows, using the 18" lengths of green grosgrain ribbon. Just above each snowflake on the pockets, fasten the ribbons with safety pins.

Note: Remove the bows when washing the apron.

Sugar Cookie VASE

Fill this unique wool and wool felt Sugar Cookie Vase with a few of your favorite things—dried or silk flowers, festive decorations such as sprigs of holly or simple evergreen branches, or lots of holiday candy!

FINISHED SIZE: APPROXIMATELY 8" X 13"

INGREDIENTS

Yields 1 vase.

2 fat quarters of green houndstooth hand-dyed wool for outer vase

1 yard of moss-colored wool felt for lining and vase base

11" x 11" square of buttercream wool felt for sugar cookies

8" x 8" square of lemon wool felt for cookie icing

22" x 36" piece of heavyweight stiff interfacing

2 yards of fusible web, 24" wide

2 skeins of size 3 red pearl cotton

2½ yards of red-and-white striped grosgrain ribbon, ⅝" wide, for ornament bow

Embroidery thread for piped icing

Thread for construction

10" x 10" square of tear-away stabilizer

Seam sealant

Fine-tipped permanent marker

Freezer paper

Temporary spray adhesive

CUTTING

From the red-and-white grosgrain ribbon, cut:
4 pieces, 22½" long

SUGAR COOKIE RECIPE

Prepare four Sugar Cookie Ornaments (fronts only) using the instructions on pages 7–8 as a guide. Set aside.

PATTERN PREPARATION

1. Using the marker, trace the outline of each vase pattern (pages 92–93) onto the *uncoated* side of the freezer paper. Separately trace a pattern for the interfacing by tracing the dashed lines of the patterns. Cut along the lines of all traced patterns.

2. Using a *dry* iron, press the larger freezer-paper patterns, *shiny* side down, onto the moss-colored felt and the smaller patterns, also *shiny* side down, onto the interfacing. Cut on the marked lines. Reuse the patterns as necessary to cut a total of four vase sides and two vase bases from the felt. Cut four vase sides and one vase base from the interfacing. Also cut four vase sides from the houndstooth wool in the same manner using the larger patterns. The patterns can be reused several times. If the patterns are not reusable at this point, you'll need to create new ones before cutting the pieces from the houndstooth.

3. Apply fusible web to the front and back of the interfacing cutouts. *Do not* remove the paper backing at this time. As you work, remove the paper backing from the cutouts before fusing.

SIDE CONSTRUCTION

1. Center and fuse the interfacing cutouts to the wrong side of the corresponding houndstooth wool cutouts. Fuse the base interfacing to one of the moss-colored felt bases. The interfacing cutouts will be about ¼" smaller on all sides than the wool and wool felt cutouts.

2. Fuse the moss-colored vase sides over the houndstooth cutouts, sandwiching the interfacing between the layers. Be sure the edges of the felt pieces are aligned with the edges of the houndstooth pieces. For the base, fuse the second wool felt cutout to the first.

3. Fold the pointed ends of each vase side over by 6" and pin-mark on the houndstooth side, at the end of the point, to indicate the position of each star ornament. Pin a star on each vase side. Use a straight stitch to stitch around the outer edges of the stars close to the cut edges.

ASSEMBLY AND FINISHING

1. Align one vase side piece to a second vase side piece, felt sides together, and pin along one long edge. Using one strand of pearl cotton and starting ⅜" from the bottom edge, join the vase sides along the long edge by blanket-stitching through all layers. Stop stitching at the start of the vase point and open out the side pieces.

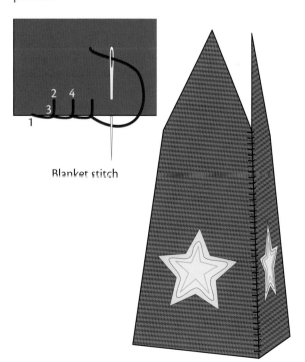

Blanket stitch

2. Continue blanket-stitching up along the pointed tip of the second vase side piece and down the other side, ending at the bottom of the vase point.

3. Pin the third vase side piece to the second vase side piece in the same manner as before and continue blanket-stitching, ending ⅜" from the bottom edge. Tie off the pearl cotton.

4. Join the fourth vase side piece to the first and third vase side pieces in the same manner to join all four sides of the vase.

5. Pin the vase base to the bottom edges of the vase side pieces and blanket-stitch around all edges of the base.

6. Fold the vase points down and pin in place, just above the stars. Tie the striped ribbon into four bows. Stitch each bow in place between the star and the vase point, making sure to catch both the vase point and the star in the stitching.

Patterns for Holly Button Plate Charger/Place Mat
Do not add seam allowances.
Trace the large pattern twice to create sections 1 and 2. Position sections as shown.
Trace the combined sections to create section 3.
Attach all 3 sections to create the full-size 13" x 13" Plate Charger/Place Mat pattern.
Or enlarge the small diagram 400% to make the full-size Plate Charger/Place Mat pattern.

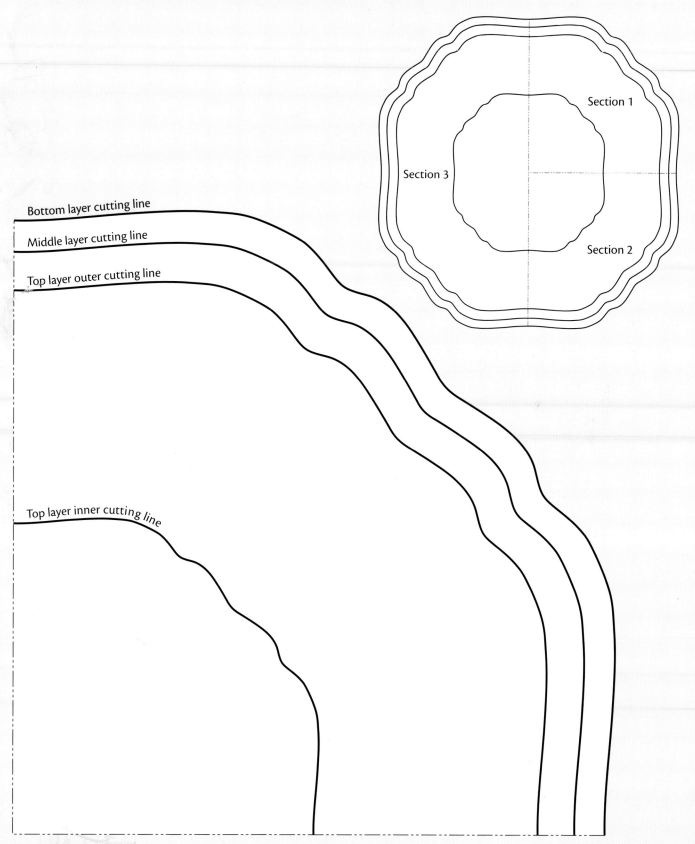

Section 1

Section 3

Section 2

Bottom layer cutting line

Middle layer cutting line

Top layer outer cutting line

Top layer inner cutting line

Patterns for Holly Button Tray/Place Mat

Do not add seam allowances.
Trace the large pattern to create Section 1. Flip from top to bottom and trace to create Section 2.
Position sections as shown. Trace the combined sections to create Section 3.
Attach all 3 sections to create the full-size 10" x 16⅞" Tray/Place Mat pattern.
Or enlarge the small diagram 400% to make the full-size Tray/Place Mat pattern.

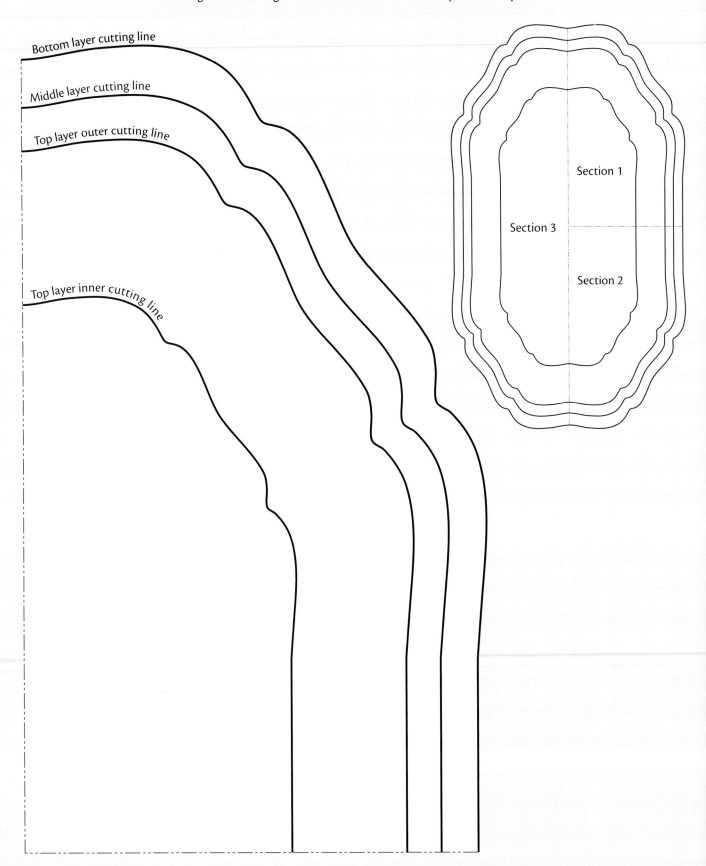

Bottom layer cutting line

Middle layer cutting line

Top layer outer cutting line

Top layer inner cutting line

Section 1

Section 3

Section 2

Pattern for Gingerbread Cookie Dough Tree

Do not add seam allowances.
Enlarge the pattern (below left) 200%.
Make 3 and tape together as shown
below right to make the full-sized pattern.

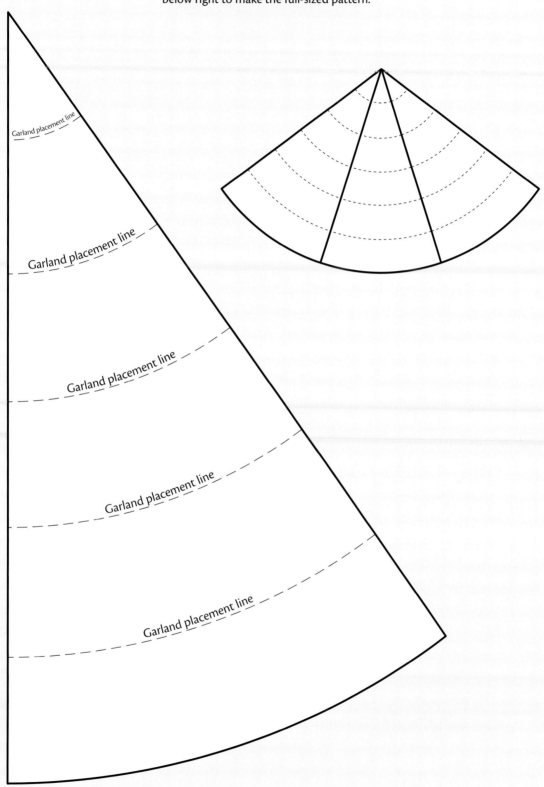

Garland placement line

Garland placement line

Garland placement line

Garland placement line

Garland placement line

Patterns for Cooling Cookies Wall Hanging
Do not add seam allowances.
Cut 1 of each of the letters.
Cut 2 stars.

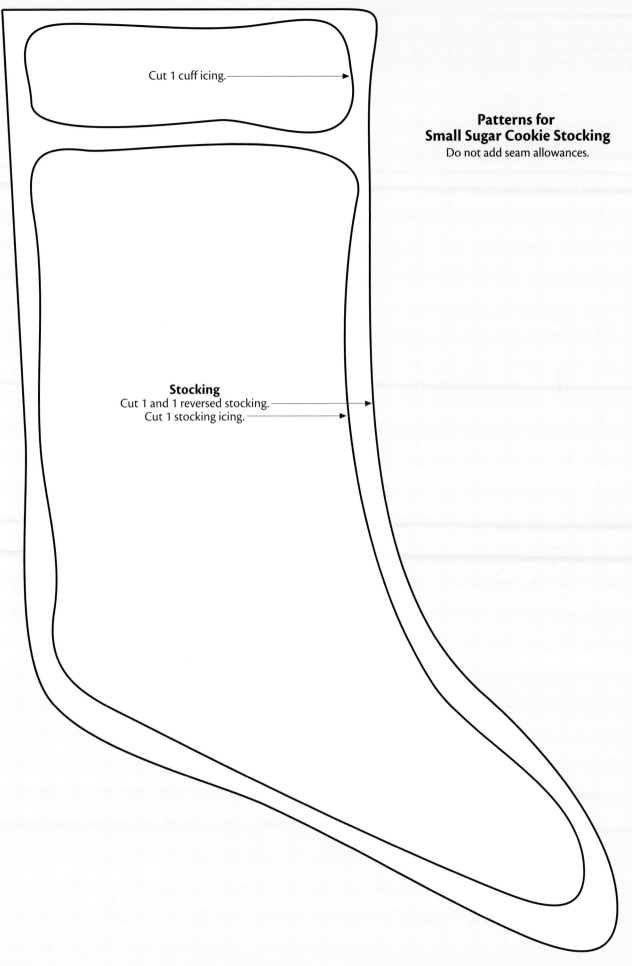

Cut 1 cuff icing.

**Patterns for
Small Sugar Cookie Stocking**
Do not add seam allowances.

Stocking
Cut 1 and 1 reversed stocking.
Cut 1 stocking icing.

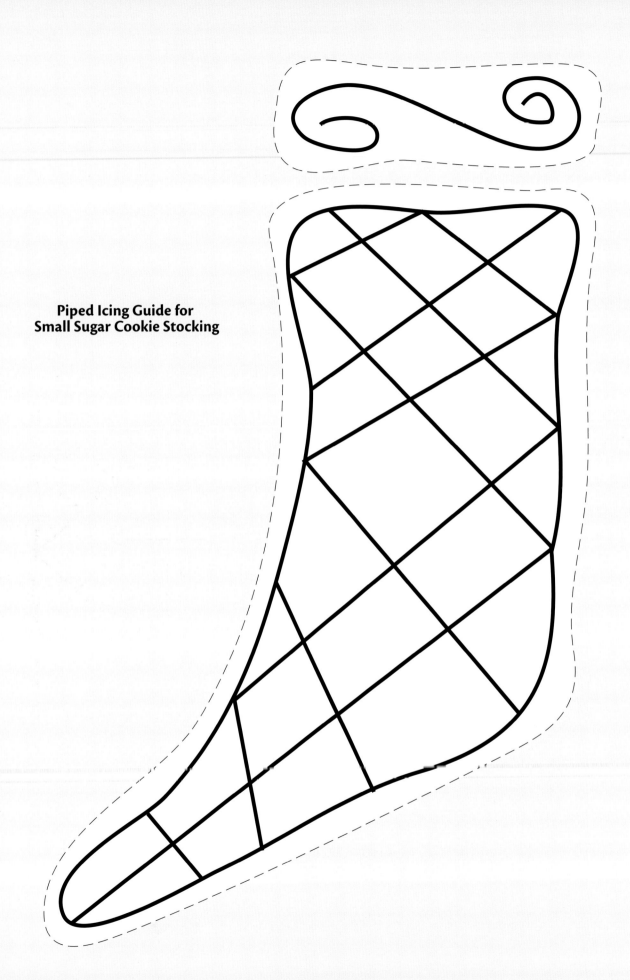

**Piped Icing Guide for
Small Sugar Cookie Stocking**

Patterns for Gingerbread Stocking
Do not add seam allowances.
Enlarge patterns 250%.

Stocking
Cut 1 and 1 reversed.

Piped icing guide

**Patterns for Ginger Cookie
Punchneedle Ornaments**
Do not add seam allowance.

**Patterns for Sugar Cookie
Punchneedle Ornaments**
Do not add seam allowance.

Button placement

Use these numbers to make a new
sugar cookie ornament every year,
or to celebrate a favorite year.

**Patterns for Sugar Cookie
Punchneedle Ornaments**
Do not add seam allowances.

Button placement

Button placement

Patterns for Ginger Cookie Lined Apron

Do not add seam allowances.

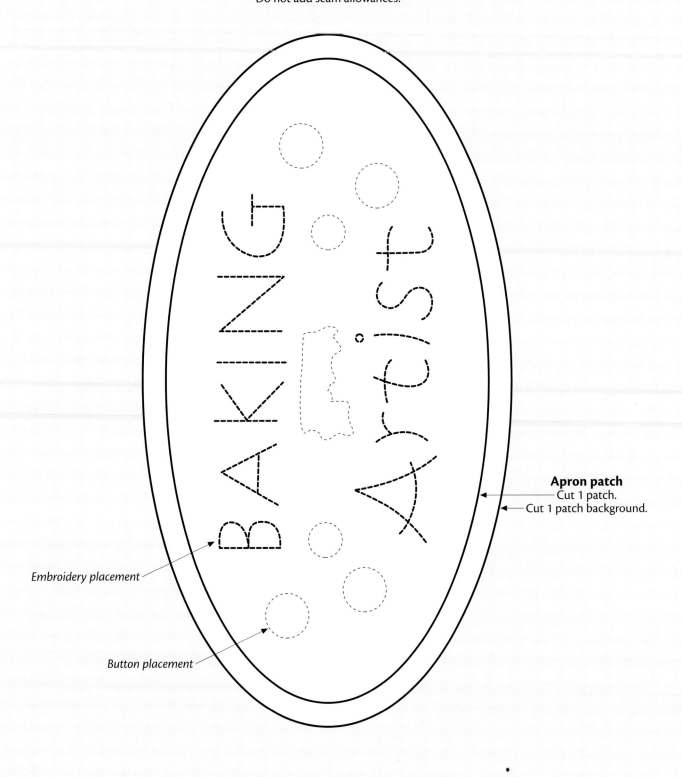

Apron patch
Cut 1 patch.
Cut 1 patch background.

Embroidery placement

Button placement

Pattern for Sugar Cookie Vase
Enlarge pattern 125%.

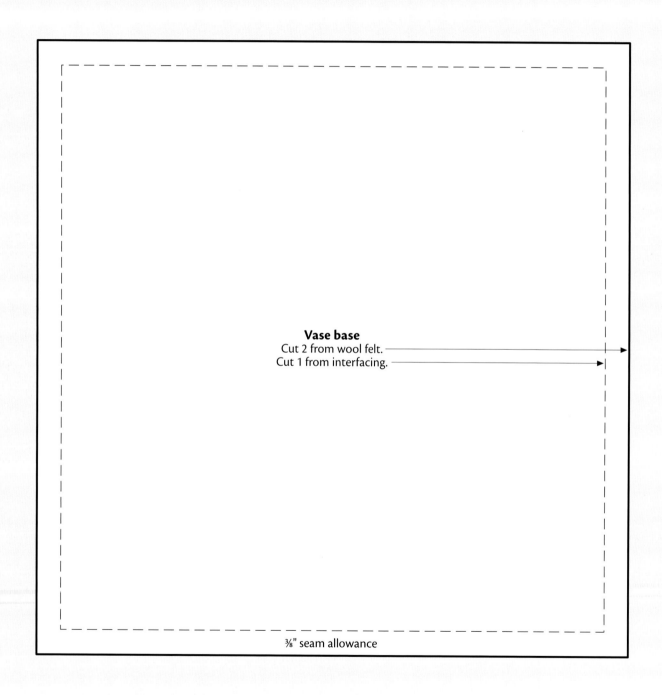

Vase base
Cut 2 from wool felt.
Cut 1 from interfacing.

⅜" seam allowance

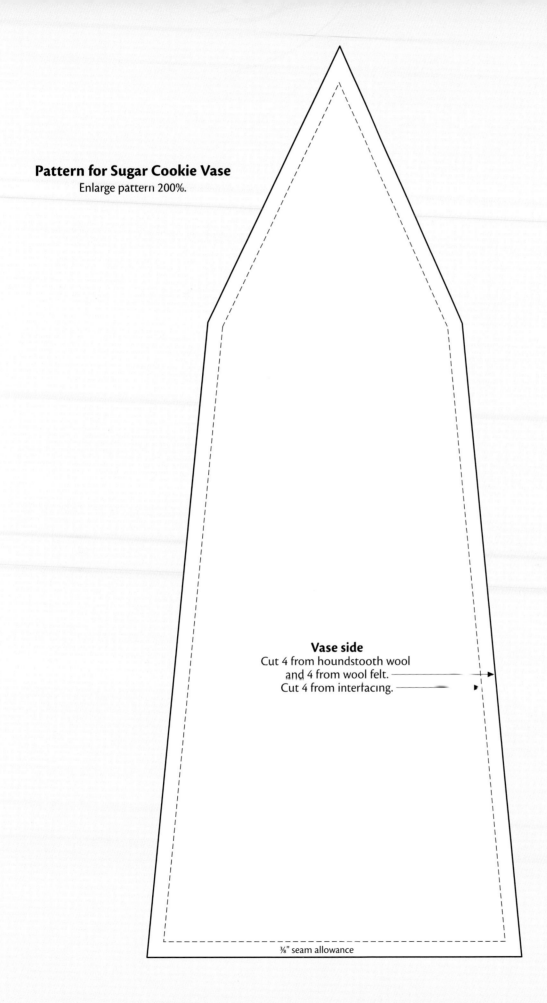

Pattern for Sugar Cookie Vase
Enlarge pattern 200%.

Vase side
Cut 4 from houndstooth wool
and 4 from wool felt.
Cut 4 from interfacing.

⅜" seam allowance

SOURCE GUIDE

While I encourage you to create your own Artful Offerings projects in any way you wish, I find that some of my customers like to make their creations using the exact materials I used. This source guide will help you find the products showcased in this book.

Artful Offerings
www.artfulofferings.com

The entire Artful Offerings pattern and book collection, as well as collaborating partners' materials used in this book, can be viewed on our Web site. In addition, a variety of fine sewing, quilting, and punchneedle patterns are available for purchase online or through local quilt and needlework shops and sewing centers. While visiting our Web site, check out the "Designer Alliances" page where we've linked the logos of each of the companies listed below to their individual Web sites for fast and easy access.

DMC Corporation
www.dmc-usa.com

Web site displays the extensive line of distinctive DMC threads. Click "Store Locater" to find a retail location near you.

Homespun Hearth
www.homespunhearth.com

Carries the entire collection of Artful Offerings designs online, as well as kits and many of the materials for your favorite Artful Offerings patterns.

Just Another Button Company
www.justanotherbuttoncompany.com

The "Locate Retailer" button on this site makes it easy to find a store near you that carries these charming handmade buttons.

Morex Corporation
www.morexcorp.com

Convenient spools of this company's beautiful ribbons are available in local scrapbooking and craft shops and online. Click the "Contact" button on the Web site to find a store in your area.

National Nonwovens
www.woolfelt.com

Available in many quilt, needlework, and craft shops and online through Homespun Hearth. The vast selection of wool-felt styles and colors, as well as the specific colors used in this book, can be found on their Web site.

Sulky of America
www.sulky.com

Extensive range of threads and stabilizers; click the "Retailer Locater" button to find a store near you.

Timtex
www.timtexstore.com

Interfacing and stabilizers can be purchased on their Web site by selecting "Go to the Store." Look for their products at your local quilt shops and sewing centers as well.

The Warm Company
www.warmcompany.com

Superb fusible-web and cotton batting products that are widely available in local quilt shops, craft stores, and online. Click the "Resources" button to find the "Where to Buy" information.

Weeks Dye Works
www.weeksdyeworks.com

Specializes in hand overdyed wool and fibers. They created the color Gingerbread #1234 for the ginger cookie designs in this book. Click the "Find A Retailer" button to locate a store near you.

Wrights
www.wrights.com

Huge array of prepackaged and by-the-yard trimmings; click the "Info/Help" button for "Where to Buy" information.

ABOUT THE AUTHOR

Karina Hittle and her husband, Audie, live in the breathtaking woodlands of northeastern Massachusetts. They enjoy peaceful country living and running their design studio, Artful Offerings, which currently specializes in the creation and publication of craft, quilting, and stitchery patterns "from folk art to fancy." Audie manages the marketing, business development, and sales tasks for Artful Offerings, enabling Karina to focus on designing.

By combining all the facets of art that she enjoys, Karina has developed an eclectic style that inspires the designs for Artful Offerings. She is passionate about creating an artfully fun and memorable experience for her customers, which evokes an element of excitement and surprise from the moment they first see her patterns through the entire creative process!

Besides being an award-winning quilt artist, Karina is a prolific designer and has published roughly 100 patterns under the Artful Offerings brand. She has also designed patterns and artwork for numerous magazines since founding the company about five years ago. Her designs have been featured in leading industry publications, such as *Better Homes & Gardens Holiday Crafts, Christmas Ideas,* and *Halloween Tricks & Treats,* in addition to *Fons & Porter's Love of Quilting, Quilt, Appliqué Quilts, Create and Decorate, Somerset Home, Australian Homespun,* and *Quilting Professional.* You can see more of Karina's work at www.artfulofferings.com.

ACKNOWLEDGMENTS

I believe that success is not so much a matter of where you are as it is how you got there—and how I got here is a result of the help and support of many. So it is with tremendous gratitude that I would like to thank God and also my friends and family members who have believed in and supported me on this amazing journey. Since starting the business of Artful Offerings, I've had the opportunity to meet and work with many new people who have inspired and assisted me. It's difficult to put into words how much everyone's continued support for Artful Offerings and this book mean to my husband, Audie, and me. In particular, we've had the great pleasure of working with some truly talented individuals and great sponsors. Their high-quality products make my job as a designer easier and enhance the professional look of my finished projects. Hence, I would like to extend a special thank-you to:

Miranda of Weeks Dye Works, for creating Gingerbread as a special new color of hand-dyed wool especially for the projects in this book. She responded on very, very short notice with an outstanding product that combines the highest quality and color consistency with a luscious look that's almost "good enough to eat."

Michelina and Jean of National Nonwovens, who immediately provided me with the bright and cheerful color palette of wool felt that I needed to get started working up the designs right away.

Cecile and Patti of Just Another Button Company, whose creative and whimsical buttons are the perfect touch for the projects in this book. Their generosity and rapid response to this designer's requests prove that they are more than just another button company.

Patti at Sulky of America, who generously provided all the products that make sewing possible, fast, and fun. The Sulky adhesives, threads, and stabilizers enabled me to finish the projects quickly and professionally.

Mary Ann of DMC Corporation for providing a rich and complete palette of cotton floss.

Marcus and Pam of Morex Corporation, for the beautiful and distinctive ribbons that put the absolutely perfect finishing touch on these projects.

Pat of Wrights, for generously providing me with distinctive trims that add such whimsy and playfulness to these designs.